# Soul Training
## When Healed is Only Half the Battle
## & Whole is the Goal

## Lisa E. Williams

ISBN-13: 978-0692140475

I0143059

# TABLE OF CONTENTS

# DEDICATION

*To the One who always causes me to triumph and those He's given me to do life with, especially the duo with whom I make my home.*

# INTRODUCTION

I've been a bride three times, but with only two proposals. And only one of the proposals involved a ring. With the first, I responded to the care and attention he offered me in the beginning, hoping it would erase years of rejection. The care quickly shifted to control and ended up being cruel.

With the second, I felt safe and protected from what happened with the first and from many other fears I nurtured over the years. That is, until we endured emotional distance from growing resentment, plus physical distance due to military service, sometimes for months at a time. I went from safe and protected to suffering alone in silence. Years passed before I understood the investment required for who I would become. During that time, I wore masks and make-up, living as the Great Pretender.

Finally, in the midst of one of my most heart-wrenching performances, I walked off stage. Going against everything I believed in, I packed up and moved out of our home five years into my second marriage. Broken and ashamed, I hoped to regroup and return as the girl he asked to marry him six years prior. That would erase the feelings of failure, right? Wrong.

I needed an intervention in my soul.

Determined to find the right fit in a man, I'd lived my entire life trying to become irresistible so that my relationship investments wouldn't be returned to me again. I strove to engage my audience while avoiding the mirror. Failure accompanied a belief that grew up with me and lived with me throughout my adulthood: I'm not good enough.

In my world, I shared my all in relationships with men, but settled for pieces in return. I didn't demand much, and any requirements I had were coupled with low expectations. With the bar set so low and my personal investment so high, it would seem that I could experience an enduring relationship, no matter how unfulfilling. However, the problem was I hadn't uncovered the root of my unhealthy habits.

Why did I sabotage romance with handsome, attentive guys only to welcome the chase and uncertainty of spending time with the aloof ones? If he was attractive and smart, why didn't I believe he could really care for me?

Turns out I couldn't see my way to loving others in a healthy way until the girl in the mirror was healthy.

So, what do you do when you realize you're emotionally bankrupt, going through life giving your version of love from an empty well? Perhaps a better question is how to know when you're emotionally bankrupt.

I thought I had it all together, spending much of my down time learning and practicing ways to become a better package for the people in my life, especially the men. I wanted to feel the warm, fuzzy type of love everyone seemed to have, except me. I wanted what every love song on the radio, every movie and television show had. I wanted the Huxtable family dynamic and The Facts of Life friendships. Instead, I had my life, which was trending in the opposite direction of a happy ending.

When I moved out after five years of marriage, our dog Hershey went with me. At the time, I worked from home and was Hershey's primary caregiver, so it only made sense. Plus, Hershey was the object of most of my affection since joining our family a year prior.

As I learned about Hershey and he learned about me, our interaction began to rehabilitate my heart. My first lesson was how I wasn't as great of a communicator as I thought; I realized that some of my relationship breaks were due to miscommunication, not malice. Hershey showed me how to embrace differences and not hold onto mistakes. Since he couldn't ask questions or apologize, I learned not to read too much into Hershey's messes. There was no benefit to rubbing his face in it, no matter what people suggested. Translating the ability to give similar benefit of the doubt to my human interactions changed my narrative about friends. Rather than walk around with my tail between my legs feeling defeated, I could assume they were loving me their way, taking assumptions of malice off the table.

After more than 10 years of ups, downs, and transitions, I'm still learning from Hershey. He made it easy to say "yes" when my now-husband, Jeffrey, asked me to marry him. Accepting my ring during his proposal meant more than changing my name and giving "it" another try. Finally, I was ready to make a sober decision rooted in a commitment to continue saying "yes," day after day, year after year, no matter what.

I know dog people get it. And I understand those who think I'm nuts since I wasn't always a dog person. Though I'm okay disagreeing with you, I wrote this book for you as much as for dog lovers. I've been getting the comments and looks for over 10 years, so I'm aware of how strange this bond seems. Before, I didn't have the words to explain. I do now.

In the coming chapters, I walk you through the journey of how Hershey helped me to see "me" so that I could understand my needs and prioritize them to ensure my love came from a full well. Each of our souls is made up of our emotions, intellect, and will. Therefore, broken souls affect everything we do, including how we speak to and care for ourselves. When we don't properly care for ourselves — inside and out — we are prone to destructive behaviors that affect us and others. Prioritizing our personal needs as part of soul training is a service to God as much as to self; this process opens the door to true love.

Soul training is a process meant to:

- Prepare you for radical change in your thoughts and emotions
- Push you beyond your comfort zone and fear levels
- Promote you to a higher level in the way you operate in life and relationships

Soul training is about repair and restoration of brokenness and soul wounds. It is making an intentional, focused effort to renew our minds to the truth of what love is and allow that truth to govern our motives and actions. Love begins with God, then us, so loving others comes out of how we love ourselves. When I make the effort to invest in myself, I won't let someone wreck my investment. But, when I'm more concerned about someone else than me, I'm likely to mistreat me for that person…and inevitably, at some point, I mistreat the other person.

Soul training isn't about self-glorification. It's about prioritizing ourselves properly for God's purpose. According to Ephesians 2:10[1], He has a purpose for each of us. Neglecting ourselves is like putting the child's mask on first in a flight emergency. Our ability to fulfill our purpose diminishes every time we misinterpret what we should do first. When we allow our souls (will, thoughts, emotions) to drive us, we don't allow the Spirit to flow through us freely, hindering God's purpose from being fulfilled in our lives.

While your struggles may not mirror mine, I hope you'll join me on this journey, chronicling my emotional growth and relational success after engaging in soul training with Hershey. While I don't have all the answers and have made mistakes on the journey, I know how to course correct now. This training helped me learn to identify when I get off-balance and need to get back to basics.

Are you ready to get onboard?

---

[1] *For we are His workmanship, created in Christ Jesus for good works, which God prepared beforehand so that we would walk in them. (Ephesians 2:10 New American Standard Bible)*

# 1 | GROUND RULES

The mid-afternoon drive to potentially choose a puppy was the beginning of my journey toward a type of open heart surgery. Soon I would follow a path of paw prints leading my heart to a joyful freedom I could barely fathom. While married at the time with a number of great friends, I had a void inside. Rather than acknowledge the lonely suffocating feelings of unworthiness creeping up in my heart, I chose to wear a mask.

Using overt expressions, I let everyone around me know how much I loved them. In many ways I lied to myself and others because my affections arose from a needy place. Although I knew about God's love for me, I couldn't feel it. So, I showered people with what I was missing inside, hoping to receive a tangible love in return. My unwritten principle of life was to offer high investment, with low expectation, and low risk. This pattern frequently left me out of balance.

My "life math" simply didn't add up. Scattered throughout my past — and some present — were heartbreak, rejection, and broken friendships. If my life was the example, I wasn't learning many life lessons. While I thought I was getting a puppy to simply fulfill my ex's request to add a pet to our family, another plan eventually unfolded.

The plan was for a puppy to show me who I really was and help train me to a new way of relating to myself and others. Why? So I could experience the parts of life I was missing. Interacting with Hershey, I would learn to see myself in a new way. The new lens would eventually be the gateway to learning the role I played in my life's mishaps.

After driving over two hours, my ex and I arrived to meet our perspective chocolate Labrador retriever puppy. Thankfully, we both knew instantly that he was coming home with us. We also agreed to name him Hershey. Once the paperwork was complete, we hit the road again. Unfortunately, no one properly prepped this super cute ball of mocha-colored fur with the blue-grey eyes for his long car ride, so he wasn't a great passenger. We had to pull off the road several times to clean the effects of his car sickness and calm him down. I was grateful for the break from the car when we stopped to pick up puppy supplies!

While the little creature and his car sickness was still growing on me, he was a hit with everyone else he met, even in the pet store parking lot. People approached us so enamored with his fuzzy face and puppy breath that they kissed him in the mouth. Uh yeah, about that — nope. They had no idea that his "sweet puppy breath" was actually the result of vomit from an hour prior! Needless to say, my puppy love was off to a slow start.

The more time I spent with Hershey, the more he grew on me. In the beginning, I tried to avoid getting sucked in by the puppy eyes and whimpers. Nonetheless, mere weeks later I succumbed to the puppy conspiracy. I went from a rational, sober thinking woman to a dog mom. Baby talk and all. He even went from "the puppy" to "my sweet Hershey bar."

In the human love department, I didn't try to hold back like I did with the pup. I usually opened up pretty quickly. Unfortunately, moving quickly meant I was often unaware of how people felt about me initially. I thought my bubbly personality was inviting and acceptable. A closer look at the verbal and nonverbal responses I received suggested that I was a nuisance. I began seeing eye rolls, facial expressions, and body language showing people's true feelings. Once I discovered that body language didn't always match the words I heard, I weighed my options. I could either try harder or pull back. Most times, I'd try harder.

Often, the input I received from social cues dictated how I felt about myself. If I got smiles and laughs when telling a story, I assigned a level of worth to those reactions and endeavored to be even funnier. Everything I said, wore, thought, and did pointed to my need to be accepted.

In time, the experience of tangible, unconditional love from my puppy knocked down a wall in my mind. His puppy love broke me from the idea that delivering a worthy performance was the only way to guarantee love. As I trained him on the rules of dog-human engagement, this cuddly, unassuming puppy soon took over as my trainer. He began to help me decipher how to see and handle myself to provoke the love I needed.

Before I knew the extent of what he would bring to my life, Hershey began to steal my heart in spurts. Within a few short months after bringing him home, I was completely smitten. The pup we named after a chocolate kiss was in my life for a reason, even if I didn't know for what. Mildly obsessed, I started taking him everywhere. Suddenly, the intermittent feelings of emptiness showed up less. I began to use him as a substitute for loneliness and he became more than a companion.

When Hershey first came to live with us, it was several months after my then-husband returned from a year-long military deployment. I was in my early 30s and still quite insecure as I navigated my second marriage. We were experiencing difficulty reconnecting and I felt more alone than when he was away.

Soon I began pouring all my attention and affection on Hershey as an outlet from our tension. Twelve months later, we were on the brink of marital separation and I felt invisible. Invisible and, by default, unlovable. I spent many evenings sitting on the floor, my face wet with tears of emotional turmoil. Those nights Hershey crawled into my lap licking my elbows or playing with a toy. He became my comforting companion, the best at getting me to smile when tension squeezed breath from my lungs.

By this time, there was little talking with my husband unless it had to do with meals or the dog. We passed each other day after day in cold silence. We had remodeling work going on and contractors spent days tearing down and rehabbing much of the inside of the house. Our lack of intimacy and communication intensified my feelings of rejection. The construction seemed to mirror in me what was being done to our home — ripping out my insides.

As tension spread through the house, I became more and more dependent on Hershey to prove I was alive and relevant. His need to go outside persuaded me out of bed each morning like the aroma of coffee. His cuddles were my solace at night. For months, that was our life.

As I acknowledged all the ways Hershey enhanced my life, I sought ways to repay his loyalty and unconditional love. I wanted to take him anywhere I went, and also expose him to a life resembling doggy royalty. I dreamt he'd live as a welcome family member with toys and treats everywhere. Though I was fully prepared to spoil him rotten, I decided training would be the best way to serve his needs and mine. His projected size and strength made training a non-negotiable investment. It was my responsibility to give Hershey a foundation of training that would make everyone's life easier (since his breed is known as much for mischief as for brains).

While adult Labs can be well behaved and docile in service as seeing eye dogs and more, many start out as rambunctious, often destructive puppies. These puppies grow quickly, need consistent training, and have astonishing jaw strength. Without redirection and training, it's amazing what they perceive as chew toys! Uninformed owners can be surprised and perhaps overwhelmed by the amount of work it takes to raise these pups and some abandon or return them.

I don't have a clue how and why people would feel they can return an animal for behavior problems without having invested in any training. I'd driven hours to get Hershey and take him from his home. He never asked to come with me. I felt I owed him something. Even so, I didn't anticipate the mutual benefits of my decision to invest in his training.

Early on, I loaded up on books, articles, and television programming about dogs. I'd been around dogs, but Hershey would be the first puppy I raised. Although all the marriage books I read didn't seem to help in that area, I hoped to get dog ownership right.

All the trainers agreed: dogs need firm, consistent, positive reinforcement training. In particular, Labs need focused training because their 'puppy brain' lasts long after they became full grown physically. So, their potential to knock someone over or destroy furniture grows faster than their brain development. I had my work cut out for me. Hershey needed ground rules if we were going to make it through the puppy years in spite of the close bond developing between us. At four months he was getting big, growing into those huge paws. Time to get busy.

Hershey's first trainer was Debbie Bickford along with her dog Nigel. We encountered them at a puppy preschool class at Tucker Pups, a training facility in Chicago that also did grooming and doggie daycare. Each week I showed up more than an hour early to feed and walk Hershey outside in hopes of lessening the chance that he'd be "that dog."

Which dog? The one barking incessantly because he wants the treat and cares nothing about learning how to earn it. Oh, and the dog who inevitably walked to the center of the room and pooped while the trainer was talking. (We avoided most, not all, "that dog" episodes).

In the beginning, watching Debbie train with Nigel was a lesson in humility. Nigel basically dropped any toy like it was on fire to run toward Debbie the moment she called his name. Even when he rolled around with the puppies, the world stopped for him when she called; he responded immediately. Debbie didn't have to yell (unless all of our puppies were really loud) or call twice. After watching them, I went home wondering if Nigel was part robot. My dog couldn't stay focused on me for more than 10 seconds and that was pushing it.

Prime example: I'd throw the ball and he'd run to go get it. Someone else in the park or at the beach threw a ball to *their* dog. Hershey would drop the ball he just retrieved for me and off he went. Over and over, I had to wrestle other dogs' toys and balls from him and apologize to owners. I thought maybe I'd be better off finding out where I could buy robot parts like Nigel's.

An early point Debbie stressed was the importance of training to the point where your pup's responses are reliable, no matter the distractions. Did she realize the meaning of preschool? Had she met my puppy? Even with her detailed instructions, it was a lofty goal. Still, I believed there was a key to unlocking the door to a well-mannered, well behaved dog. I just had to find it.

After watching Debbie and Nigel for a few weeks, I saw a potential answer to the mystery of his obedience - their relationship. She said once, "Your dog should think you're the most important thing in his life." That's why it didn't matter what Nigel was busy doing when she called; she was most important to him. In the same way, Hershey's reliability depended on our relationship. I shifted some of my focus from textbook suggestions for teaching Hershey to obey to finding ways to build our relationship. Our relationship priority — me first, everything else second — became the first ground rule.

Many books and articles suggested one way to build relationship is through walks. Sounds like a no-brainer, right? Our parents were right. Nothing worth having comes easily.

In the beginning, walks were intended to build relationship, tire Hershey out, and prevent potty accidents. If I didn't drain some of his energy, Hershey drove me bonkers running around looking out of each door and window he could reach, and barking at something as innocent as leaves falling from the trees. Early on, we walked farther and faster than his little legs wanted to go. When I tired him out he took naps. Long, quiet naps.

I'm aware there are numerous ways to build relationship with a dog, like playing and feeding. In the beginning, though, we needed more than what playing in the yard could accomplish. So, whether I felt like it or not, I got out and walked Hershey.

In time, I loved walking Hershey. Except we lived in Chicago. And he needed walks in January, just like he did in June. Chicago summers are beautiful, but often short. The winters are long while spring and fall can be hard to distinguish from winter. All the same, whether sunshine, rain, sleet, snow, frigid cold or fierce winds, Hershey and I braved them together.

Even before Hershey and I moved out, I was the primary care giver due to work schedules. Since I managed to keep Hershey's walk times pretty regular, he quickly grew reliable enough on the potty front to have free reign of the house in our absence. When Hershey had the rare accident, it was often by the door as if he waited there to see if anyone would show up before it was too late. Even though he didn't make it every time, we had another ground rule — your restroom is outside — under our belts. Score!

With that ground rule established, the motive for our walks shifted to reducing boredom. Much like genius children, Labrador retrievers need exercise and stimulation to avoid destructive habits.

To prevent boredom, a few times a week Hershey and I drove to do our walks in different areas with more grass and dogs than our neighborhood. We also went to doggy festivals, parks, beaches, and numerous pet stores to create adventures. I hunted for the most durable chew toys and constantly added to his supply. The result? In our more than 10 years together, Hershey only chewed one strap off one shoe. That's a dog any girl can love.

As Hershey grew stronger, our walks grew more interesting, and another ground rule emerged. In her foundational training on walking our puppies, Debbie stressed that our pups should walk loosely on the leash without pulling. She often repeated there should be no tension on the leash, and our dogs should be beside us or only slightly in front. Meanwhile, I was convinced that Hershey was part Alaskan Husky, bred to pull sleds. Our next ground rule centered on Hershey walking beside me and not pulling.

If I previously made our walks sound like Hershey didn't head for the border every time we exited the car, readjust your mental picture of those early walks to something way more flustered. If you saw us in the early days, your conclusion may have been, "Poor dog. That lady doesn't know what she's doing!" Maybe you spotted us on a day my Houdini pup saw something beyond his reach and shimmied his way out of his harness to run after it. If so, you likely shook your head in disgust watching me chase him down the side of a busy street. Not a pretty picture.

However, it was us. We were learning each other, establishing the ground rules that helped make him the amazing pooch he is today. We set the stage early with rules like, no jumping on the table, no growling at me or guests, and no biting. And don't run into the street or drag me into it either.

Stopping at the training basics would've done us both a disservice. We were prepping for a deeper exchange. From me, Hershey learned a new language and ways to navigate a world of unfamiliar territory. From him, I learned what it meant to undergo soul training. More than a companion, Hershey ended up being much like a therapy dog. I thought we established ground rules for him so that we could coexist peacefully, but more than coexistence was in store.

Beyond our ground rules, this book is peppered with many of our training lessons and results. The foundation of communication Hershey and I laid is necessary for any relationship. We're different species that discovered ways to relate even though we don't speak the same language. This is a vital skill. Just because someone loves you, doesn't mean they're equipped to speak your language. Therefore, some training is in order!

By nature, dogs are masters of learning our words and understanding our emotions. Over time they can even anticipate what we need, making them excellent companion animals. Ideally, we do the same for them. As you read through the training adventures of Hershey and me, I hope you find that you can relate, whether or not you have a dog. On the journey, I learned that God had ground rules for my relationship with Him and others. My best life depended on me grasping His rules. This book outlines my transition as I embarked on a soul training journey by learning the ground rules and following commands.

# 2 | SIT!

One winter afternoon Hershey was attacked in our condo building by a female Labradoodle named Charlie. Fresh off a rousing, snowy play session with a huge Golden Retriever, Hershey walked with me several windy blocks back home, welcoming the warmth inside the foyer. As we headed for the elevator, I noticed Charlie down the hall with a couple of my neighbors.

She glared at us for a split second before taking off in our direction. Her owner calmly called after her, not thinking the situation was urgent. With fire in her eyes and swiftness in her step, Charlie completely ignored his calls. Fixated on my pup, whom she normally couldn't get to because of her leash, Charlie was free and on a mission. Hershey stood straight in front of me with his tail high and stiff, ready to protect me from the approaching tyrant. He glanced back at me as if to confirm: 'I got this.'

Stunned, I let his leash go. We had nowhere to run to avoid this encounter, and I didn't want to complicate the situation with a tangled leash. When Charlie reached us, Hershey made quick work flipping her onto her back and pinning her on the floor. By wrapping his mouth around her neck without exerting any pressure (though I didn't realize that right away), Hershey had made his point: 'If I wanted to, I could demolish you.' He let her up and backed away, moving closer to me. His performance and restraint impressed me. Amazed and proud, I could've kissed him.

Unfortunately, our relief was short lived because Charlie wasn't done. Furious at Hershey's domination, she lunged for him as I nudged him behind me with my knee. (Mind you, it seemed as if her owner was moving in slow motion. How long was this hallway?) Mouth wide, Charlie continued to lunge; my protective instincts moved me forward, so her teeth sank into my thigh rather than my pooch. I was ready to explode. I grabbed Hershey's collar as Charlie's owner finally reached us.

Unable to answer his questions about whether we were okay, I stomped around the corner to the elevator. Thankfully, it was on the ground floor, so we got right on. Out of a mixture of relief and frustration, I cried quickly on the way to the third floor. By the time we got inside and I peeled away layers of jeans, long underwear, and tights, I found a bruise in the shape of Charlie's teeth, but my skin was barely broken.

A worse revelation came the next morning.

Though he had no outside scars, the encounter changed Hershey in deep ways, invisible from the outside. Somehow, I guess he felt he failed his mission to protect me. I had no clue Hershey even knew Charlie bit me! I learned a lesson that day, though it didn't click until later. Hershey handled the situation between the two dogs and backed away. When I intervened, I got bit and it shifted the dynamics of the outcome. It's not always a good idea to intervene in a situation we aren't invited into, even with the intent to help. Aside from a minor dog bite, from that day, Hershey's new mission was to shield me whenever we stepped out of our door. No dog could get close; big or small, near or far.

Our neighborhood was peppered by dogs in every direction, so Hershey was nearly impossible to walk after encountering Charlie. He'd get so worked up that he would get up on two legs, growling and snarling at dogs down the block. Like a jealous lover, Hershey communicated that I was off limits. Repeatedly, I explained the situation to neighbors. My sweet dog changed after an attack. Finally, I found a trainer who could help. He told me exactly what I needed to do and said it shouldn't take more than six weeks to retrain him. It all hinged on one of Hershey's first lessons: sit.

I didn't know much about dog behavior before getting Hershey, but once he was home, I did some research. A puppy's early childhood years occur during the first eight weeks of life. Around week six, Mom goes from "milk machine" to "disciplinarian." Unfortunately, puppies have become a business, so many puppies are removed from the litter at or before week six. At that age, they no longer have Mom to correct them or their brothers and sisters to help them navigate their place in the pack and establish their identity.

Without crucial training from their litter mates, puppies' social skills go undeveloped or underdeveloped. The problem may be unnoticeable initially. When the pup grows up, consequences can appear in their behavior into adulthood. When Hershey came home with me at seven-and-a-half weeks old, he was one of two dogs left in the litter. I knew nothing of how age-related issues related to dogs. But having skipped most of second grade, I totally understand the concept. While I looked like the older kids academically, socially I was still pretty awkward. I was ignorant about relationships and social cues on top of being anxious and overly chatty. The only thing I needed to learn more than when to speak, was when to just sit and be still.

In first grade I stood out academically. (Which was code for finishing my work quickly and disrupting all the other students). The teacher's solution was to approach my mother to ask whether I could join a second grade class for part of the day. My mother agreed and I began to get in less trouble with the extra work and moving between classes. And I was extra prepared when I entered a new school the next year.

Working at a higher level the prior year caused my work to stand out in my new school. By October, the teachers and my mother agreed to let me finish the year as a third grader. There was a small problem with my new status. I didn't have a clue how to fit in. My book smarts didn't equate to maturity.

Hershey as a puppy behaved much like me, the third grader in a second grader's body. My new status on the playground — third grader — didn't come with instructions. Naturally, I tried to find an "in" with the older kids which opened the door to my becoming a proficient people pleaser. Similarly, Hershey's size suggested he was more mature than his brain or behavior exhibited. He needed to be trained more in certain areas. Without encountering one of his bad habits, it was impossible to know that he'd been removed from the litter too early. We each had ways of hiding our shortcomings in a crowd.

The first command books and classes often recommend for puppies is "sit." It's described as a foundational command to help address a puppy's short attention span. Sit helps promote focus and position a pet to prepare for what's next. Also, it's hard for puppies to get into trouble when their bottom is on the floor and their eyes are looking upward.

Hershey learned to sit early on in our puppy preschool days. The trainers suggested beginning by placing a treat above his nose. Then, I kept raising and guiding it backwards toward the back of his head. As his nose went up, his bottom had to come down or he'd fall over. As soon as his bottom hit the floor, he got the treat. Even though I was up against an attention span that seemed to only last a millisecond, the command worked like a charm once I figured out his motivation: yummy, smelly treats.

Hershey and I worked hard on the sit command in those early days and we practiced constantly. He soon associated sitting with having good things happen. All I had to do was hold whatever he wanted just out of his reach. So by the time the trainer told me about going back to the sit command to address his protective aggression, he was a pro and I was hopeful.

The trainer explained that I'd have to put Hershey in a sit position and desensitize him to the passing of other animals. In other words, as he sat we would work to retrain his thinking away from seeing every other dog as a menace. I had to remind him that as the alpha, it was my responsibility to discern and respond to danger. His role was to sit and allow me to lead him.

In the situation with Charlie I hadn't performed well as an alpha in protecting the pack. My response bred uncertainty in him, which led to aggression. His aggression made me uneasy. My uneasiness fed his uncertainty and reluctance to allow me to be in control after the incident. We were in a cycle that we'd have to unravel to resume a healthy relationship. To move forward he needed to sit while I refocused his attention and reestablished his identity as a part of my pack.

Why was Hershey's identity important to his development? The same reason my identity as the third grader in the second grader's body was wrecking my development. Taking time to get a solid fix on who we are and where we belong helps eliminate the doubt and fear feeding our unhealthy behaviors. Hershey's doubt and fear about my leadership pushed him to try and control the situation whenever we went out. My own doubts fed my desire to "make" everyone like me.

Revisiting my first lesson for Hershey after the attack ended up being his first lesson for me. In response to my sit command Hershey instinctively looks up. Initially, it was about what he wanted — a treat or toy, for example. Without some type of reward or further instruction, he lost focus. In other words, without an exchange he didn't remain engaged. My animal instinctively demonstrated that the best relationships require input from both parties.

(Who's the trainer now?)

In all my years, I'd kept my expectations low and had no frame of reference for positioning myself to receive. Content with being the doer, I didn't understand how to sit back and allow people to respond to me. Much of my time was spent observing how my deeds were being received by the other party. I rarely noticed their responses to not being offered a platform to reciprocate my feelings in their own way.

Within the process and practice of teaching him to sit, Hershey showed me how to practice receiving, reciprocation, and awaiting instructions. I also learned to stop expecting God to respond to me before I decided whether to obey His initial instruction. Hershey said a mouthful without a word, but my walking it out required an adjustment!

Reflecting on my childhood habits of wanting to be loved and accepted, I realized that slightly obsessive behaviors were my norm. I developed bad habits of trying to get attention because of the 'need to please' tapeworm was growing within me.

Attempting to coerce acquaintances into friends, I talked and talked at school. Soon, many of my nights were spent writing lines under the covers with a flashlight so that my mother wouldn't know I'd gotten in trouble for talking...again. My mantra for those years: "I will not talk in class." By sixth grade, I was the only child who could get punished on report card day, even with straight A's. My mother simply didn't understand the basis behind my talking. Somehow, I knew she wouldn't approve of how hard I tried to make friends. She frequently expressed her thoughts on being a follower and where it would lead. She was right.

Once, I was fooling around in class playing "monkey see, monkey do" with some of the other girls behind the teacher's back. We raced back and forth from our seats to the trash can beneath the chalkboard. What made it fun? We weren't supposed to be out of our seats, so we had to be quick. Well, when Tracy* (her name really isn't Tracy) bumped her head doing it, that didn't deter me. I had to continue to rebel in an effort to defy my teacher's pet reputation.

After bumping my head, I ran to the bathroom with a hand over my eye. Already in the restroom, Tracy and friends met me with scowls of disbelief followed by choruses of being a copycat. When I moved my hand to prove my injury they began screaming. Tracy only bumped her head. I was bleeding. Ever the overachiever, I'd split my head open on the silver ledge that held the chalk and erasers. (I still have trouble making my eyebrows even because of that scar!) Undeterred by my injury or the stitches it warranted, I fell deeper into an ongoing cycle of stupid shenanigans and schoolyard rejections.

Then. Came. Boys.

I had the occasional boyfriend growing up, but the majority of the guys I knew fell into the category of friend. My aggressive tomboy mannerisms carved me a secure niche in the friend zone. Guys told me all their secrets for years. If only my inside information could've helped save me from high school heartbreak or that of my first two marriages.

In relationships, I established a precedent. I was content with the act of giving everything with little opportunity for the other person to engage me or even know me. I hadn't taken time to acquaint myself with my likes and dislikes enough to share them. While I never would dish out food and treats to Hershey all day because I knew he'd become fat, sick, or both, I didn't withhold treats from the men in my life. Somehow, I didn't fear making those relationships unhealthy. Instead, I encouraged their taking everything I dropped at their feet while allowing them to be lazy in their interactions with me. Though I noticed a cycle, I had no game plan to break free. The fear of being forgotten made me strive instead of sit. No matter how 'sick' it made our interactions or how sad it made me, I replayed the tactic year after year.

Where did this behavior come from? How did I become so aggressive in my need for love?

Remember Hershey's behavior after Charlie's attack? His doubts about my ability to protect him made him fearful and aggressive. My self-worth was attacked by the ways I felt alone and rejected as a child. Changing classes and schools disrupted my ability to make friends and begin to establish my identity. I felt alone and fearful. Where Hershey leaned toward negative aggression, I erred on the side of people pleasing with a vengeance. Having missed certain social skills before being placed in an environment with children older than me, I couldn't easily discern between my false perceptions and the truth. So doing things to make people like me became my norm.

Sadly, the older I got the less effect my tactics seemed to have.

After my ex and I officially separated, Hershey and I had time alone. When I could see myself without any distractions, the lies I once told myself laid fully exposed. Those lies dictated my emotions and often led me to quit on myself and others. The break-up was the next in a number of soul wounds that remained unaddressed and influenced me to create behaviors to shield my heart. My mouth said I wanted to be loved and invited people to me. My actions betrayed my request and were loyal instead to deformed ideas of what I thought love looked and felt like. I chased people who were indifferent and superficial. I either pushed away or ran away from the people who were real.

One day the command being issued to me finally became clear. I felt the tug on my heart to quiet myself and SIT: Study my Inner Tendencies. In a moment of quiet after crying, wondering why this kept happening to me, I began to see. When I took a moment to pause, I could hear God more clearly. Sitting with Him also meant sitting with me. Sitting meant learning who I am and seeing my potential. Seeking opportunities for growth. What was His specific instruction to me during our quiet time together? He let me know that in order to make progress in the right direction I would have to stop hiding and allow my heart to be exposed. The more I took time to sit — not complain, not cry — the more truth replaced the lies that were a part of my belief system.

Sitting taught me how love requires strength, commitment, compassion, and a vulnerability that begins with me. The need to control others by showering them with gifts was a sign of weakness and fear. Fear that I wasn't worth being loved just because of who I am.

Loving myself was foreign, but God commanded it as a prerequisite for loving others well. My quest for lasting love inspired me to press on toward learning the truth. I had to lean back into a sit while looking up for the next instruction or an exchange. It wasn't easy.

Sitting also revealed that my ability to love and trust

were warped. I thought I was easy to get along with and submissive. However, at my core, I held the belief that relationships were about control. Thinking I wanted to be controlled, I was obedient and pliable, changing into whatever my environment required.

Unintentionally, I gave my heart and soul in the form of indulgence. Indulgence is primarily one-sided and holds little danger of rejection. Engaging in sharing and vulnerability wouldn't allow me to squash certain pieces of who I was inside. But my habit was to hide certain parts of myself to hopefully guarantee love and acceptance. In other words, I wrapped manipulation in a box with a pretty ribbon.

Even my reflection in the mirror opposed me in my fight for loving myself. I began to see bits and pieces of my value peeking out from behind a cover of insecurity based on my weight. Fat? Not really. Just not as skinny as most of my friends. Comparison, a waste of time and energy, was self-love's newest threat.

Once again, Hershey's training doubled as my teacher. To get rid of restless energy, he'd demolish a chew toy. Hershey laid there and went to town with the chew toy and would fall asleep soon after. Like Hershey, I had to find a different way to expend restless energy so that I could sit, regroup, and receive the reward of a renewed mind concerning my relationship with myself without basing my self-evaluation on anyone else.

To begin, I had to acknowledge that my issues began and ended with me. As a child who was unsure of herself and began looking for ways to manufacture love, I developed a mindset that stood as a monument built by wrong choices, painful experiences, and unhealthy interactions. That mindset was the root of many of my broken relationships. Not my weight. Not how I looked, or what I didn't "give up" to please someone else.

Great. I found the source. But these were long-held beliefs. How would I manage my emotions until I gained the strength to refuse to let others' opinions determine how I felt?

First, I needed to realize that the issue was in my soul.

Pain had generated thought patterns founded on lies. Those lies made it into my personal philosophy and perspective. That's how soul wounds penetrate. The pain I hadn't dealt with properly went down beneath my emotions and infected my soul. Then I began to respond to life from that soul wound. Behaviors born out of soul wounds grow deep, strong roots. This is why it's important to forgive and release people who've hurt us.

My relationships resembled a revolving door. The socially awkward third grader grew into a woman of low self-esteem with a trail of broken situations. To be healed from my wounds, I needed to forgive others and realize my capacity for love was based upon my ability to see myself as God sees me. Nothing else.

Sitting and reflecting on how deeply I was and am loved by God opened me up to new possibilities. I noticed where I had given people a platform in my heart and allowed their thoughts and opinions to challenge what I knew about God's love for me. I had to remember: 'God is not man.'

Never in my wildest dreams did I think I'd develop courage to not only love, but be loved completely. I lived with a daily fear that I'd never measure up to who I believed I needed to be. My form of "sitting" was focusing on what God offered me in relationship and engaging my faith to receive it. Just like Hershey looked to me, fully convinced of his worth and my power to fulfill his needs, I had to know that I was worthy of what God had for me. So, I planted myself in front of Him where I could finally grab hold to the truth that lifelong love wasn't beyond me because He loves me best.

God doesn't hesitate to engage with me. He recognizes and welcomes me when I make time to sit with Him. He's never too busy to go over and over a point with me until I am assured that He can be trusted or I am loved, whichever is plaguing me that day.

We all have the opportunity to exchange love and trust for fear. When your peace of mind is threatened, I encourage you to sit. That, my friend, is what God wants from each of us.

When we're about to spend money or binge eat because of hurt feelings, it's time to sit.

When we think vengeance is our right, it's time to sit.

When we lash out before we listen, it's definitely time to sit.

When we voluntarily sit before Him and present ourselves, we can rest assured that God will respond, and the pain, fear, and even entitlement we feel will pass. He's never intimidated or put off by what we bring unless it's pride, unbelief, or fear because they reveal a lack of trust. If we continue to pacify ourselves with treats until certain feelings pass without letting God intervene, we tie His hands. He won't intervene without our faith.

I had to sit until I could wholly trust.

When I sit, I'm at peace in a safe, familiar place. God never thinks, 'You again?' Nor does He require me to try and clean up before I come to Him. He knows I can't. He welcomes my ugliness because it means that I've finally stopped trying to hide from Him. God shields me from the devourer and rains favor on my interactions so that when people meet me, they see Him. He enables and empowers me with grace to do mighty exploits, like be in a healthy marriage, have healthy friendships, and pursue my dreams.

Teaching Hershey to sit reminded me of the value in choosing to be still. Just like Hershey, I will never grow out of needing to sit. Sitting demonstrates a position and posture I can return to again and again until my inner critic is silenced, any fear is erased, and my faith is renewed.

Today, I can definitively declare that God has no intention of leaving His children with emotional voids that prevent us from reaching the truest height, depth, and width of who we are. He is relentless and known to accomplish His purposes in unexpected ways. Often, the process will be misunderstood by those on the outside. We can go through life embracing where we are and Who's on our side. Or, we can spend our days attempting to explain what others were never meant to understand.

Shifting into a more self-aware perspective requires real work of putting a mirror up to your soul. Walking by faith and not by the sight of all your shortcomings — perceived and real — is a journey.

We must continually practice loving ourselves so who we present to the world is whole. When we start with dependence on God, He helps us define the nature of wholeness as an individual. Sitting with Him can fuel your ability to love yourself. And you can be creative in how you "sit." Whether you sit with a journal and a pen, stand with a canvas and brush, or take a walk in nature, the point is a posture of laying yourself open for an exchange. Allow His perfect love to evict fears of not measuring up to the picture of perfection in your mind.

My biggest "sit" lesson? God's intent for our relationship with Him is to be an exchange even though we can't ever repay what He has given. Similarly, we are responsible for requiring the people in our lives to reciprocate. We weren't created to only give and give. We're not serving others well by letting them off the hook when they consistently overlook our relationship needs. No more lowering the bar to help people qualify for continued access and relationship.

Learning to sit is also about valuing time. We shouldn't allow people to occupy our space and time out of obligation or pity. Reserve your time for your people. The ones who won't ask you to apologize for being too "you." Those are your people.

As you read on, take time to reassess your friends and relationships. Release the fear of losing, and trust that the right people will remain. Beware of limiting your ideas based solely on your past experiences.

Like Hershey after his encounter with Charlie, you may assume everyone wants to attack, and that mentality will make you tough to engage with. Sit until you're prepared to raise the bar for yourself and your relationship standards. As your standards shift and your perspective changes, you'll likely find yourself with a new friend or two. Don't be afraid to "train" them how to treat you.

### Soul Training Tips

- Without proper training, the consequences of underdeveloped social skills appear in our behavior.
- When we sit, we make time to <u>S</u>tudy our <u>I</u>nner <u>T</u>endencies.
- God doesn't intend to leave us with emotional voids that prevent us from reaching the height, depth and width of who we're purposed to become.
- When you assume everyone is out to get you, it makes you tough to engage with.
- Don't be afraid to raise the bar for yourself and others in your relationships.

# 3 | STAY!

At 16, I asked my boyfriend to marry me.

To me, he was beautiful, which was a plus. Doesn't every girl picture her babies before making such a commitment? We met during the Christmas break of my senior year of high school and his freshman year of college. The night we met, I was working the drive-thru at McDonald's handing out the food.

One of my coworkers warned everyone via the headset that two cuties were coming through in a gold jeep. Lots of squeals about how fine they were followed her announcement. Another worker attempted to snatch their food away from me to get a closer look. I promptly snatched it back and walked over to the window, fully expecting to not be impressed. Unfortunately for me, I was really impressed.

Under normal circumstances my flirtation skills were outstanding. Today I could only smile. The guy in the passenger seat was smiling back. Inside, I screamed at myself for not listening to my mother. She'd yell about how I didn't care enough about my appearance when I went to work and one day, I'd regret it. I saw no need to look cute to hand out burgers and fries. As with many parental warnings, "one day" had arrived.

Thankfully, my smile was all the encouragement he needed. They circled back through the drive-thru a second time to get some water...and my phone number. I stood there with the same grin plastered to my face when he asked my name and whether he could have my number. My manager had it ready for me to pass it to them so we could get back to business. For months, he didn't call. Then, one evening in May, I picked up the phone and a deep voice asked to speak to me.

"This is she." He asked if I remembered him from Christmas break. I did.

I calmly asked if he could hold and ran to my mother squealing, "It's HIM!" After my quick explanation of who "him" was, she rolled her eyes and told me to calm down and go finish talking to *him*.

That weekend, we had our first date. Soon after, he became my everything.

Though I was only 16, I hungered for connection, and more than anything, I wanted forever. I had a high school sweetheart my last three years of high school and we'd been crazy about each other. We went through typical teenage break-up phases. One week we were on the phone constantly anticipating the next time we'd get together, the next week it was over. Again. No surprise, we always ended up back together.

Eventually our different backgrounds and parental restrictions prevented us from getting more serious, though we always remained friends. By the time I met Mr. McDonald's, I craved a more tangible commitment. I wanted to know someone would always be there for me. (And that we'd have beautiful babies.) I also wanted to be part of a big family. Holidays with his large, close knit family are some of my fondest memories of those years. I longed to make the warm experiences of those family gatherings permanent.

It wasn't to be. We broke up too. Part of the blame lay in my ever-growing insecurities. Who could blame me? Girls literally yelled their phone numbers at him in the car, suggesting he call them after dropping me off! Ignoring them, he'd grab my hand or kiss me on the cheek, but those moments stuck with me.

On top of that, we were young and attended college in two different states. The phone calls became more and more one-sided until I couldn't pay my calling card bill anymore. By midterms, the letters stopped. Desperate, I went to visit and it turned out to be the beginning of the end. Missing my flight back and having to stay an extra day began to unravel the final thread we hung by. I never knew for sure, but I think he did some magic to avoid me running into his on-campus girlfriend.

As is often the case with love at 16, I never got my 'happily ever after' with him.

Though I remained friends with most guys I dated, a seed of rejection lay burrowed deep in my heart. That seed was watered by feelings of being unwanted with no one willing to fight for me. As a result, rejection grew in me until the water wasn't enough. The seeds began requiring food. What was once a little seed of rejection took over my heart, strongly craving acceptance and companionship.

Over time, I went from merely asking people to stay to begging and bribing. My self-esteem faltered and took my expectations along for the ride downward. From that wreckage, I got a bright idea: disconnect from the potential disappointment of break-ups and rejection. How? Quietly accept scraps from people in my life. Take whatever they gave and be content.

Somehow, my worth dictated to my brain that I could get by on scraps. No complaints. No high hopes that may one day shatter in disappointment. Take what you get. How did I get here? The second grader who'd been tossed in with third graders was now a teenager in college with "adults." A tough cookie in some respects, but so naïve in relationships. Like a lamb in a den of lions.

I didn't date much during my college years. No one would come near me because of my age freshman year. My second year and I'd accepted Christ. I figured I was better off keeping my distance from the opposite sex since relationships usually meant I lost part of my senses. I'd run up phone bills and boxes of letters, while my answering machine and mailbox remained empty. I resorted to matchmaking and third-wheeling, going on dates with my friends and their dates. In retrospect, that may have been an opportunity to learn a few things. Only I had no clue how to change.

After graduation many of my friends went on to pursue graduate studies and a couple even married their college sweethearts. Me? I had no plan and no man. Back home I went.

I stuck with the bribery to get and keep company. I dated some, usually as the pursuer. In addition to phone calls and letters, I now had the means to drive-by and even drop off slow-jam tapes. Making many mistakes and learning few lessons.

Nearly every relational move I made was plagued by emotional decisions that were doomed from the beginning. From ill-fated matches and dangerous liaisons all the way to my short-lived first marriage at 26. Things were slightly better by the time I was remarried over five years later, but the root cause of rejection lived on. Therefore, the behavior persisted into my 30's.

That's how Hershey got a piece of the dysfunction.

I found myself almost idolizing him. Although I couldn't articulate it in those early months, the way I placed him on a pedestal spoke for me.

Watching another marriage slip through my fingers, I desperately needed someone to choose me. Fight for what we had. Stick around for better or worse. Stay.

Like most training commands, stay goes against everything a dog naturally wants to do. When I open the door, Hershey wants to greet my guest. When I go into the place where all the food and treats live, Hershey's nose tells him to follow. And why should he stay put while I greet another dog? The "stay" command comes off as a barrier to everything yummy and fun.

In the dog training world, stay is used as a safety precaution similar to having a little one pause to look both ways before crossing the street. The desired result is for the pup to freeze. To further complicate things, the pup shouldn't move from the stay position until he's given a release command or gesture.

Since a puppy's world looks totally different outside the confines of the home or yard, he or she needs help staying safe. Stay is all about maintaining a position irrespective of the animal's desires. There could be a safety element attached, or the command could be part of a drill.

My beloved Hershey seemed to have an attention span of a millisecond. I thought he would never get the hang of stay and wait for the release command. But despite my complaints about his attention span and focus, I had to admit some similarities in our behavior. When I met someone new and God wanted me to pause until He released me to go deeper, I often missed it. If I'm honest, many times I showed the patience of a gnat.

Was I ambitious to expect perfection from Hershey? Yep. I had a lot of nerve.

After all, as a puppy Hershey basically watched his siblings disappear one by one until only he and one sister remained. Against his will, he was forced to stay behind and adjust to a new way of living.

Then, one afternoon, his human brought him out to meet us and we took him away. Where he may have wanted to stay in his current environment, he was uprooted. It was days before he stopped whining at night. The trauma of it all!

In time, Hershey stopped whining and adapted. My emotional response to broken relationships wasn't that different from Hershey's. First, I'd whine. If the person didn't come back to me, I just stalk— uh, "watched" the person who was no longer in my life. Unlike Hershey, I had control over my movements and took my time adjusting to new norms.

As Hershey settled into his new environment and way of life, his world grew larger every day and it was my responsibility to prepare him for it. The more he progressed, the more I taught him. Sit required him to understand what I wanted and perform for the reward. Stay tugged on his emotions to complete the skill.

After recognizing me as his new "person," Hershey followed me around. Room to room, he always seemed to be under foot. A part of me loved the attention, so I never encouraged any boundaries in this area. I later learned how codependent behaviors hinder training.

After allowing Hershey to be with me constantly, all of a sudden, I asked for the opposite. In training him to stay, I wanted him to sit or stand in one spot while I walked away. Without the ability to reason or the foresight to understand the purpose, I asked him to adjust his habit. And his habit was tied to a person (me). What prepared him for this? Could he know for sure that I'd be back?

Think about that for a second. Have you ever had to deal with watching someone walk away from you? Deep down, you hoped they would return. Because if not, their absence would mean your financial, physical, and emotional investments weren't enough. That you weren't enough. Even if some parts of you were relieved because of incidents and issues between you, many times, a measure of pain inevitably accompanies loss. In all your humanness, you struggle with rejection or release after loss, especially if you haven't been trained in ways to effectively process emotions.

By humanizing Hershey, I didn't realize at first how much I asked of him in these training sessions. Though I was fluent in the practice of letting myself off the hook when things became tough, I stood my ground in his training. I prioritized his wholeness over any momentary discomfort, even when I rarely did that for myself. To succeed with stay, he'd have to process my temporary absence in a healthy, balanced way.

We started the training with me putting Hershey in a sit. One hand held a treat near his nose and the other made a 'stop-in-the-name-of-love' gesture as I said "stay." I'd repeat it, taking one or two steps backward. The times he didn't move during the steps, I'd yell, "Good boy!" and present him with the coveted treat. Then, we started over again. With each repetition I increased the space between us. Every time Hershey didn't follow me, he got praise and a treat. As usual, he was a rock star.

We started in the living room and progressed to other rooms in the house. This lesson was one we practiced by playing hide and go seek. I told him to stay and hid toys for him to find. Soon after, we moved the party outside.

For more real-world practice, I'd leave Hershey on

one side of a street and cross it, telling him to stay. I'd have someone hold his leash, and he'd cry loudly until I was close to him again. Even if he really liked the person with the leash, he whined. If possible, Hershey would've run into the street after me. Seeing me wasn't enough. My proximity mattered.

Before Hershey could fully grasp the command and calmly watch me move away, we had to create pattern to help him 'know' I'd come back. Repetition and reward were our methods for building trust. In our relationship, trust would result in obedience. In the beginning, when Hershey whined and squealed, I discovered I couldn't comfort him and expect him to get the lesson. We both had to hang in there until the end when it all became clear.

After some time, Hershey trusted me enough to endure separation. As he grew older, I could drop his leash and throw away his poop bag on the other side of the street without him moving. As long as he could see me, he was content. He'd watch intently, and perk up when I came back.

As our trust relationship grew, a shift occurred. I would issue the command; Hershey would stand there for a moment, then calmly lie down. Imagine that! He trusted me enough to rest, though I moved farther and farther away. He didn't chase me or put his emotions on display in an attempt to manipulate me to move in a different direction. What a concept! But, what grade would God give me in a similar situation? I'm sure I wouldn't qualify for a treat.

Isn't it funny how much insight we get on lessons when we're not the pupil? The mere fact that God had to add Hershey to the cadre of teachers in my life shows I needed special attention. More times than I can number, I felt like God moved away from where I was. Unlike Hershey, I didn't chase Him. I went after other distractions and comforts instead. (Just ask my waistline!) When I couldn't find a distraction, I hung out by myself waiting for the pain to subside. It took years to discover that positioning myself before God and staying there was what I needed to revive my soul.

Being battered emotionally by human rejection made me doubt what could be accomplished in spending time with God. So, I avoided the only One who loves me unconditionally. I ignored the tangible ways He wooed, comforted, protected, and restored me after all the fights and break-ups. Couldn't recall the numerous times He rescued me from the brink of disaster.

The irony of avoiding God? I usually moved in the direction of someone with no desire to be with me. I chased old feelings rather than receiving what was reserved for me. God has time and answers for everything we need. He's after the wounded places in us that automatically reach for people. In my case, I even reached for Hershey when I couldn't get to a human.

Despite all my years of knowing and loving God, I relegated Him to a deity who wasn't concerned with my emotional battles. I had no experience reaching for Him to wipe my tears. And I also kept my distance just in case He was disappointed with my mistakes. I had no desire to confront my own problems, let alone allow Him to confront them.

What was the basis for this fear-motivated behavior? I didn't want to be alone, or worse, abandoned. Giving a part of myself to someone who could exit my life at any moment gnawed at me. But I didn't have the power to make a man, or even a friend, stay with me. My lips said, "Stay." Meanwhile my heart screamed, 'Beware! At some point, this could hurt!' And I pushed people away, hurting them and myself in the process.

Sure, certain relationships needed to end. Absence doesn't always equate to rejection, and separation isn't always a bad idea. Emotions blur the line between the two. Even when my brain discerned the need for a boundary or separation, my heart betrayed my brain. My heart craved human presence. The outcome: emotional push and pull.

Fear of abandonment and underdeveloped coping skills caused me to squirm and miss the cues I needed to make adjustments and work at a relationship. Since fear was at the root of many of my soul's issues, I had to start there. To be whole, first I needed to figure out the source of the fear jockeying for attention in my soul.

Why was I so uncomfortable with distance between me and someone I loved, and why did that automatically introduce insecurity? After all, Hershey matured and learned to rest, "knowing" I would come back for him. So, why in my thirties did I continue to struggle with people leaving my life?

During Hershey's training, I only gave treats when he calmly waited for me, exhibiting trust in me and his training process. Yet, I expected God to dish out treats without me offering trust. As a full grown woman, I resembled a puppy: immature, sitting for a split second, then running toward comfort.

Little did I know then that when I don't trust God, it's impossible to truly trust myself. If I don't trust myself, I approach others with similar suspicion. If only we had a way to identify our relational deficiencies to give people the choice not to engage. At least then, potential friends and mates would have an idea of what they were in for!

My second objective after finding the source of my fear was to learn healthy confrontation. Despite all my known and unknown flaws, thankfully I had some friends who made me feel safe enough to cry, complain, confess, and even confront.

Imagine driving along a dark, country road at night

and a deer jumps in front of your car. You know the swerve you make as you slam on the brakes, nearly crashing into a tree? That's how I avoided confrontation. I'm from Chicago, so a more appropriate example may involve dodging potholes in the winter. With the vast number of potholes on the streets, you either choose to slow down and adapt, or potentially derail your entire trip by blowing a tire.

I was so used to dodging dialogue that I derailed several relationships in one of two ways. First, rather than say what bothered me, I'd pull away quietly. My vehement opposition to rejection said, 'Don't rock the boat.' Or, if I had trouble getting over some negative feeling or occurrence, I made it my issue alone. No need to discuss it; I decided I just needed to forget it and move forward.

I'm sure many of the conversations I avoided cost me more time and relationships than I even realize. Sigh.

This was my way of protecting myself from rejection and the wrath of people who may not appreciate my opinions. I developed a philosophy based on keeping the peace. Suppress my desires, disappointments, and disagreements at all costs. While I thought I was giving others what they needed, I betrayed my own needs over and over.

I carried that "tip-toe-on-pins-and-needles" philosophy with me to work, church, and all my interactions. I made it a practice not to ask questions. Questions rocked the boat. Instead, I learned to watch environments like a hawk, which helped me learn to anticipate needs and assist like a boss! However, what brought accolades outside crushed me inside.

Even so, I nurtured the "tip-toe" seed for nearly 30 years. Feeding on disappointments so tangible that my physical weight ballooned. As divorce number two approached, I was extremely out of touch with who I was. Broken, I didn't resemble the old me, inside or outside. Often, I ended up avoiding pleasure with the same vigor of avoiding pain.

Ultimately, while I fed my fears I worked against what I said I wanted most. Hershey had learned to trust that even if I moved away, he could stay and expect my return. But my losses of friends, boyfriends, and even spouses altered my way of being. I coped by coming up with possible scenarios of how I was at fault. Make the reason they left be about something I was, rather than something I wasn't. To me, only one of those felt like rejection.

How could I grow beyond the point where my self-sabotaging ways threatened my desire for connection? More than 15 years after proposing to my boyfriend, my soul's brokenness had matured along with my age.

Hershey and I had already modeled the order of things I must do to move in the right direction. First, I had to *sit*. Study my habits and figure out the patterns I kept repeating. Then, look up and await God's next instruction.

The instruction? I had to *stay*.

I had to plant myself at the feet of Jesus and learn from Him about the Father who sent Him into the earth to redeem me. He plucked me from obscurity and placed me in my mother's womb, knowing my potential full well. The tighter I held onto my own way, the more I added to my distance from God. Isn't that what Jesus came to erase? I had to learn to be at peace, allowing Jesus to "drop the leash" and seem to move away from where I was. Then, rejoin Him and walk in the path and direction of His leading.

Jesus spent time in unfamiliar surroundings with far less than the heavenly amenities He knew. He did so with His lineage and identity intact. The sacrifices required to fulfill His purpose didn't sway His commitment, nor did the behavior of those around Him. He was steadfast. I had to make Him the standard.

Staying means I resisted the urge to run from pleasure or pain. No placing demands on people's emotional or physical presence. Both were in direct opposition to where I endeavored to go.

When friends shook loose from my tight grip, I needed to allow God to show me my role in the chaos I was calling friendship. Before He could retrain me, the girl in the mirror had to really see herself and learn how to clean up her act. Prior to leaving Hershey on the other side of the street, I trained his behavior in the living room. Smaller quarters afforded us greater focus. To get the real picture, I had to be willing to focus and allow God to point out my missteps.

And that He did. Soul training is about finding root causes of behavior and changing in order to move toward next level living. For example, God showed me how I did a poor job of taking my ex along on my growth journey when he returned from deployment. We'd been struggling to reconnect even before we brought Hershey home. After 14 months apart, we were almost like strangers.

Disappointments I thought I'd forgiven lingered in my heart. I became impatient with his coping mechanisms as he tried to readjust to home life. We disagreed often as he noticed my independence from handling things on my own so long in his absence.

It seemed neither of us left any room for change and growth in our relationship equation. Then, the physical separation due to military and work commitments created an even greater emotional gap between us.

In the thirteen months after his return from Iraq, we went from reunited to living like roommates. So, I started planning to run from the rejection and abandonment I believed was coming any day. In that time and mental space, I didn't see another option. In my assessment of the situation, he was indifferent and didn't care if I stayed or not. I decided not to stick around and lose the fight and more of myself.

Additionally, I still carried avoidance habits, which kept me from asking the hard questions. In my view, there were valid reasons to leave and valid reasons to stay. While it was my habit to run away from conflict, I hesitated because I didn't want to get divorced again. Eventually, I chose to act on the messages I received from my ex's behavior. Every time I felt him grow colder and push me away, I died a little more inside. Against my better judgement I did the opposite of everything I wanted for my life and for us— I left.

Leaving was a mixture of pain and relief. I was relieved to be away from the heart-wrenching silence between us. But the feelings of worthlessness overshadowed any relief and cut me deeper than any words could have. Every day I wondered if staying would've been as painful as not having him run after me.

During the time my ex and I dated, we had a brief break-up. I got cold feet and disappeared. I hid out at a friend's house and didn't take his calls. He chased me. He said he understood me. Understood my fears and would always come for and reassure me when I felt the need to run. Maybe he forgot. Maybe he was going through his own emotional changes after being away for more than a year. Either way, he didn't come, and it nearly destroyed me.

Remember the guy I proposed to at 16? When I saw him moving away, I didn't feel worthy to ask him to stay. But his mother and I had become close. She had adopted me as a part of the family and treated me like her own daughter. When holidays came around, I had a seat at the table back with the family. I showed up every time. Part of me was always ready, just in case he changed his mind.

Years later, here I was retreating again. I was a pro at running away when hurt invaded the place where love once lived. I convinced myself I was doing the other party a favor by running. In reality, my unwillingness to submit to what God was developing in me was my downfall. Whenever I gave away my power, sat on my opinions, or sidelined my dreams, I lost myself. And refusal to maintain my identity in relationships had consequences. I paid the price multiple times for what I was afraid to address.

On that painful journey during and after our separation, the image in the mirror Hershey held up before me started becoming clear. Alongside pictures of growth, I could see images of dysfunction. Back then, my life proved to be the direct opposite of stay and wait, but I was in training. By allowing God to show me the extent of my dysfunction and the consequences of running away, I developed hope in my potential to have a healthy relationship in the future.

What about you? There isn't a one-size-fits-all remedy when it comes to processing through moments where we feel abandoned. Having a dog as a companion filled a need for me, but I had more work to do. Tuning into needs beyond food, water and exercise opened me up to a world where I could learn from Hershey. For you, it may be a counselor or new friend who can explain and expose a way of life you don't currently see as an option.

The key to your transformation is how you approach your need to take a moment.

When words hurt like daggers and you want to hide, stay. Recognize that God is where He's always been and feels the way He's always felt about you. I have been guilty of gross misperceptions about God's love for me. My pride suggested that I was up against unique obstacles that few could understand. By the time God allowed me to see my circumstances for what they really were, I was embarrassed. False comparisons were robbing me of opportunities for gratitude and growth. And I fell for it.

My life had some tough moments, sure. Some were beyond my control. Other times I contributed to the turmoil. But when I take the sum of my experiences and recognize that they add up to the life I get to live today, I give thanks.

When situations you're facing threaten your ability to

move forward, pause. Don't run away from the issue or your part in it. Make it a priority to get beyond the pride that suggests you're the only one who experienced what you're facing. Find ways to give thanks and have hope.

Running away never accomplished what I anticipated. I had to learn to stay and face the music. My encouragement to you is to stay. Work at entering into the rest of God.

During creation, God didn't see the need to continue working on the seventh day. He'd been recording His results as He went and things went well. So, during His time of rest, He wasn't preoccupied with the idea that unless He continued to strive and intervene, the world would fall apart. His rest on the Sabbath modeled for us how to let go of the reins sometimes and just be.

The root of my transformation lay in exchanging fear and unbelief for abiding trust. Fear caused me to run. I had to go to a place in my inner code to correct the error where I decided God was like man. I made space in my heart for a revival of faith. I rooted fear out of my soul and got reacquainted with His faithfulness.

Trust gave me permission to rest. To stay and rebuild.

One of my greatest "accomplishments" has been my ability to move my comfort out of the top ranked place in my life. Maturity enabled me to learn the ways of building strength and strong foundations. Developing muscle strength requires muscle strand breakdown. Building strong foundations require tearing up existing foundations and digging deep. Comfort isn't part of either of those equations.

Moving beyond surface-level living required me to take a new stand. Instead of hiding my head in the sand, I chose to stay in uncomfortable places and process through situations I would've previously avoided. I intentionally re-installed a foundation for trust to rest upon.

My toughest behavior shift was from the busyness of running whichever direction fear dictated. How? By taking my emotions and relationships off the throne of my heart and placing God there. With Him in the driver's seat, I saw patterns and signals I missed when I drove every situation.

Is your life pointed in the direction toward a life you love? Perhaps it's time to relinquish control.

Pull over.

Stay a while.

Allow God to chart the path for the next leg of your journey. Your heart is safe with Him. He loves restoring beauty from brokenness.

### *Soul Training Tips*

• Absence doesn't always equate to rejection, and separation isn't always a bad idea.

- The tighter we hold our plans, the more we perpetuate the distance between us and God that Jesus came to erase.
- What you avoid because of fear will often cost more than you're prepared to pay.
- Manipulation may guarantee presence of people, but won't guarantee the presence of love.
- God resting on the Sabbath should demonstrate for us how to let go, rest, and let things be.

# 4 | SPEAK

I love to read. In books I find comfort, an escape, instruction, inspiration, and more. However, string together some of the same syllables verbally, and my nerves of steel melt into a pool of anxiety.

*"I need to talk to you."*

Those words sparked anxiety in me like no other phrase. Whether in school, at work, or chatting with a friend, swarms of butterflies would take over my stomach and any appetite would vanish. Tears would hover, as I anticipated the worst possible outcome from words. That wasn't always the case.

I seemed to exit the womb talking. I was proficient at mimicking others and saw no issue with repeating any- and everything I heard. I'm told I could be heard stringing together "adult phrases" in my room as a toddler. Apparently, I picked up a few things, here and there, during my naps that coincided with my mother's phone calls. Reprimands and correction came quickly since my repeats usually came at inopportune times.

Later, I used better discretion, yet remained divided between who I was inside and who I pretended to be.

By the time I hit high school, I was a full-fledged actress. By day, I was a super friendly student and cheerleader. Once off school property, I was an insecure, fearful nerd. In four years, my performance earned me a diploma, a stint as Homecoming Queen, and acceptance into some great colleges.

I said and did what was expected of me faithfully. When I left for Oberlin College in Ohio at 16, I battled excitement and fear of change and was in desperate need of finding my voice. In the subsequent four years, I earned a degree in an interesting subject for which I had no passion. I arrived back home at 20 with knowledge, but no direction and still no voice.

My words grew less and less meaningful and weren't always truthful. My first big lie was pretending to be excited for my career prospects when I had no confidence in my abilities or education. I kept talking and talking, trying to convince myself that I was as qualified as my classmates. My ruse didn't work. I was all "bark."

Like mother, like puppy.

Imagine sitting at your computer working with a new

puppy in the house. Hershey loved to lay by the front door for hours. (Perhaps he was holding out hope that his real parents would come retrieve him.) Each passerby was like a new game. My once-content puppy went full guard dog, with loud, incessant barking warning them away. Or, maybe he was demanding they come and take him back to the farm and his parents. Either way, once riled up, Hershey was tough to reel in.

According to the experts, training the "speak" command, if done right, would mean I could quiet him quickly with a verbal command or hand gesture.

For Hershey and I, speak wasn't a cute optional trick to pull out for company. (Though when kids visit, it's the command they're most fascinated with.) I made my living working from home. When I took conference calls, I didn't have the luxury of time to find out why Hershey was barking or to calm him. When I wasn't speaking, I was forced to use mute just in case he spotted someone.

I acknowledge there are two sides to the story of barking dogs. Beyond quieting Hershey, I had to know what certain barks meant. For instance, the low growl means he smells or sees something or someone unwelcome. I wouldn't want to quiet a warning bark to a danger I couldn't see or hear. I needed to be careful not to chastise him to the point of dulling his instincts.

One evening, we were out for a walk and the pink sky

of dusk turned midnight blue blocks before we reached home. Hershey was nearly one year old and almost at his full height. He stopped to poop on a busy street, and I couldn't hear much over the sounds of cars passing us. As I bent to pick up his droppings, Hershey's leash began to vibrate in my hand. I couldn't hear his growl, but I felt it. His posture shifted into protection, and he warned the man approaching us to keep his distance.

Angry by now, the man suggested I keep my "pit bull" in check. I tried explaining how he'd gotten too close when my back was turned. He didn't care. All he knew was that my "vicious" dog nearly attacked him. I drew Hershey close and let the man pass before whispering, "Good boy."

The point? Before teaching Hershey to follow my command, I had to learn and respect his ways. I couldn't make his training more about me than him. My objectives had to align with his instincts. I had to direct his behavior, not completely shut down what he is inherently to make him into what I wanted. (Hear that, parents?)

What would that look like? My hope was that it meant he wouldn't bark at everyone that passed by, but would let me know when he needed to go outside or if someone approached the door.

Somehow, I predicted our process wouldn't go as smoothly as the one I saw on the Animal Planet channel.

I was right.

The trainer hosting the show said, 'If you can teach your dog to speak, you can teach him to be quiet.'

Really? I was willing to try anything.

The day I decided to train this command, Hershey had interrupted my work day one too many times. I didn't want to crate him while I was home, yet the barking got old fast. By now, I knew Hershey would do almost anything for the right treat. In this case, I just wasn't sure how to help him earn it.

The trainer suggested sitting my pup in front of me and pretty much going wild until he barked. Once he barked, I was supposed to say "speak" and simultaneously give him a treat.

I jumped and squealed. He sat there puzzled. I flailed more. He stared and cocked his head. Nothing.

Thankfully, before I broke a full sweat, he barked just a bit. I nearly shoved the treat in his mouth and screamed, "SPEAK!"

He seemed confused at first. But the lag time between my performance and his bark of applause shortened the next time. We were in business. (Had I videoed this little performance, we'd have gone viral!) We practiced every day for weeks and soon Hershey would bark — and quiet — with words and gestures. I felt like a genius.

While these antics are appropriate for dog training, the opposite is true in human interactions. We shouldn't have to put on a show or break a sweat to get engagement. Even so, I went from childhood chatter as a toddler to begging to be heard in my pre-teen years and beyond.

Everywhere I went, it seemed someone was telling me to be quiet. Soon, I felt unheard and unseen and, by default, unloved. Where I sought responses, I received reprimand. True to form, I retreated. Something more sinister occurred behind the scenes though. My desire to be heard revived my desire to please. Then, inadvertently, I became a liar.

Not the save-yourself-from-a-spanking lies that many of us told. (At least, I like to think we all did.) I mean the lies that diminished my heart. The lies that made my words more about the hearer than me. Lies that made me mistrust myself because I denied my pain and joined sides with the perpetrators. Little pieces of my esteem and carefree joy floated away each time I overrode my needs to satisfy someone else. Lies like:

*"It's okay, don't worry about it."*
*"I'm fine."*
*"We're good."*

Later, I graduated to giving apologies in place of receiving them. I used apologies to avoid the awkward and push past mutual responsibility. The goal? Keep the status quo. Leave no friend behind. Smiles and so-called 'happy times' were my treats. I trained myself to lose with a good attitude. Until I had no voice.

I had many friends, but my need to be seen and heard was unfulfilled. Then, I was introduced to church. Out of sporadic church visits in my formative years, I developed a love for the Word of God. Preached, written, or sung, I was enamored and comforted. All the same, I hoped someone could see behind my smile.

I lacked the courage to remove my mask and allow truth to erupt from my lips. Over time, I grew so unfamiliar with my voice and her truth that I began to believe my lies.

*"I don't need anything."*

At least that was a half-truth. I needed many things. I needed to accept responsibility for my life. I needed to stop handing over the keys to my joy and transferring ownership to whomever stood before me at the moment. I needed to stop lying about the pain I felt, even in my little group. I needed to admit how unsafe I felt and how that lack of safety prevented me from being sincere.

Generally, in watching dogs play, you'll see overly submissive dogs get picked on. A dog pack may band together to address a rude or dominant dog. However, they also band together to chase the sheepish, insecure ones into a corner. In several of my groups of friends, I resemble the weak puppy, which made me vulnerable.

God used Hershey to detect places in my soul being

fed by insecure behavior. My insecurities deposited in me the potential to be either overly submissive or rude at any given time, which meant *I* was often the source of my pain, not the friends I blamed.

One of the source behaviors that resulted in this pain? Refusing to use my voice. Most of my fear concerning confrontation revolved around things I'd rather not say.

One afternoon when in my late thirties, I visited my sister Tina. We grew up in different towns and circles, so I missed a lot of big sister mentorship in my early years. I loved when we had time to chill and chat and learn things about each other and our family. Sitting on her couch in the basement with NCIS reruns playing and Hershey curled up on the floor one afternoon, our conversation shifted to relationships. Mine in particular. She was shocked to learn my approach to relationships rested on people pleasing.

As someone who processes thoughts as I speak, I learned a lot about myself that afternoon. Tina stepped in as my "soul trainer" as we chatted about my ill-fated marriages and other relational disasters. I shared with her the ways I suppressed my true self thinking I could gain acceptance. I relayed how I began suppressing my feelings as a child to avoid making adults angry for "back talk" or whining. The fact as an adult I was still afraid to speak my truth for fear of disappointing others was unthinkable to her. Note: My sister has no problem communicating her truth any time or any place, yet she's wildly popular.

When I finally mentioned to Tina how I coveted her authenticity, she aptly replied, 'Who else would I be?' I explained how I saw the inability to be myself and still be loved as part of the reason for my divorces. Meanwhile, in her twenty-five-years-and-counting marriage, she is fully accepted by her husband who loves her as she is. Tina's philosophy? Be authentic, or don't bother.

Like Tina, Hershey was authentic and unapologetic. He had a uniform language and used it with everyone. He didn't get that from me. I spent much of my life pretending or apologizing. In school I fearlessly recited others' words and won awards and competitions for delivering them. Celebrated for sticking to the script, I decided to keep it up. I said what others wanted to hear. In return, I received plaques, ribbons, and friends.

As someone who wouldn't dare pretend and saw no need to suppress her thoughts, my sister heard my heart that day and gained insight concerning the sadness she saw in my eyes that I didn't know was there. She even got the background on her frequent question asking why I took "that dog" everywhere.

Though I didn't change right away, Tina's marital success and lifelong friendships witnessed to me that neither perfection nor pretense had a place in true relationship.

Despite my issues with developing my authentic voice, once I trained Hershey to speak, he quickly picked up ways to stress his needs and wants. He expresses desire and disappointment and isn't afraid to repeat himself if he feels ignored or misunderstood.

When he's being punished and I tell him to go lie down, he has a disappointed whine that says, 'You're mean. That wasn't my fault.'

If I'm watching television and he wants to play he has a whine that says, 'You're ignoring me.' It's very similar to the one asking, 'Do you know what time it is?' if I'm asleep or engrossed in something and his breakfast, dinner, or walk is late.

The cutest — and likely the one he's most proud of — is how he gets me to listen up.

He starts with a soft woof. *Hey.*

If I don't respond right away, he barks a bit louder. *Hey!*

Either I've brushed off the whines, or he has a physical need (like a ball rolled under the couch out of his reach and he needs me to get it).

Frequently, by the third bark, I'm standing in front of Hershey telling him to show me what he needs. People watching us are usually astonished at how trained I am. (As if on cue, he just hit me with the soft bark).

How did I come to understand what Hershey was

saying? How did we get to understand each other's whines, expressions, and body language? Our relationship had to hit a turning point. Part of training him to speak meant I had to watch and listen, and not fear his truth. Soul wounds of rejection whisper suggestions that lies are better than truth. When I believed the lie that people walked away from me when I revealed my true self, I shut her off from the world.

Hershey showed me a new way. He supplied me with different tactics to apply in my life in spite of decades of speaking fearful falsehoods. This tactic addressed my fear of confrontation. True story: barking doesn't always precede a bite. In other words, speaking up to get your needs met need not be unpleasant.

Sure, when Hershey first came home as a puppy, he barked and whined constantly. He verbally communicated insecurities brought on by his unfamiliar surroundings. Over time, I learned to discern between insecurity and urgency or desire. Each required different responses, like a trip outside versus a cuddle and a calming voice. Then, Hershey's voice changed with maturity. Getting him to redirect his energy or refocus his attention became easier and easier, and we celebrated often.

My life experience was different. As my voice changed, there were few celebrations. My romantic relationships weren't the only casualties of revealing truth. My speaking up came off as a departure from the girl my friends and longtime acquaintances knew me to be. Truth was, the safer I felt at home in my skin, the more my true personality surfaced.

After some trials and many errors, I learned to not forsake my truth for friendship. My soul was becoming whole through time with God and learning that the girl in the mirror was worth loving and knowing. I started allowing her to come out and play more often, showing off her thoughts and opinions. This "new me" with her forward approach and who no longer went along to get along brought confusion. How could my friends be sure I was being honest now? And why did I feel the need to pretend in the first place? All valid questions.

For me, the answer was easy. As I matured, I tried different things in search for the real me. Yet each time I tested a more authentic version of myself, it seemed rejection followed. Maybe that wasn't exactly the case. Nevertheless, my soul interpreted those rejections to mean the real me was unacceptable. When truth fell short of bringing people close and gaining me the acceptance I most desired, my voice faltered.

I felt this way most significantly near the end of my second marriage after a long military deployment. In his absence, I didn't go out much beyond church and family functions, so I had plenty of time to soul search, read, learn, and grow. However, since I hadn't truly developed my own voice, I also began to take on the tone of few of my friends with stronger personalities than mine.

Once the deployment ended and we reunited, he declared I changed. I saw it as a good thing. I felt better about what I was bringing to the table. More confident. Less apologetic. But how could he celebrate when some of that confidence came out in sarcasm? In many ways, I was responding to past hurts in our present conversations.

In my attempts to express to him that growth isn't the same as changing, I missed the point. I did change. Yes, maybe I changed into who I was all along, but to everyone on the outside looking in, I changed. Some changes were good; some weren't me. But because I couldn't separate the good from the bad in those moments, the relationship soon crumbled.

It took great strength to resist the temptation to crawl back and squeeze into the box I had inhabited for so long. Deep down, I knew I wouldn't fit. Going back to the old me wasn't an option. In my heart, I knew I'd grabbed hold to some things God desired for me years prior and I'd missed them chasing other things and people. So, I refused to dishonor Him by trying to go backward and possibly diminish the growth I achieved in intimacy with Him.

In that space of time, I shed fear and insecurity that suggested I lie about my needs and feelings. I learned we must leave room in our relationships for ourselves as well as our friends and partners to grow and mature. And that growth is best achieved in God's presence.

Though we hit our roughest point during the reintegration period after the deployment, we pushed on trying to make things work while tap dancing around the elephant in the room. Welcome home parties, home renovations, and getting a puppy did nothing for the brokenness tearing apart our hearts. When it seemed I couldn't fix my marriage, I continually poured energy into Hershey. In return, we developed a language all our own.

The part of me craving to be heard and relishing in the singular devotion of this animal wanted to talk all the time. I sought to prove that I was worth being listened to and even obeyed. Real change happened when I learned to honor Hershey's devotion and do it his way sometimes, tell him what I wanted without words.

Now, when Hershey wants to get me to move, he nudges my arm with his nose. He won't whine or bark unless I'm out of reach or ignoring him. If he wants an ear scratch or belly rub, he knows how to place his body within reach and lean in. I respond appropriately because I pay attention.

My love for Hershey taught me that keen observation yields relationship dividends. For years, I masked my feelings and responses, blocking true connection. With knowledge and experience came wisdom and eventually better judgment on my part. I was almost ready to open up and connect.

One year, a mentor of mine suggested that if I ever wanted to achieve true connection, I needed to find my voice. I had to stop assuming the voice of the strongest personality in the room, go back to the place where I silenced my voice, and set her free. I grabbed a spiral notebook and went to work. I wrote all the things I thought my younger self would say and what she would believe about life and love, no matter how idealistic. I also wrote personal reflections from watching people and listening closely to what they said and didn't say. As I freed my voice on paper, I slowly freed her in other ways too.

Suddenly, I could hear the difference between my voice and the other personalities I mimicked. More importantly, I learned to feel the Spirit's tug when I considered performing or putting forth someone who wasn't really me. My younger self (and her voice) wasn't just becoming free, she was maturing.

A byproduct of coming to myself was taking responsibility for my part in who and where I was: separated, depressed, striving to be happy, and stubborn. I was torn between who I was to people I loved and what I wanted them to accept from me at that time. When the two didn't reconcile, I retreated. I threw up my hands and determined it would never happen for me. I decided that authentic love from a whole place just wasn't my portion.

Sound familiar at all? Have you ever reached a place where you knew you possessed good parts, but picked up bad habits along the way and you couldn't separate them? Did you do what I did and throw up your hands? Decide to live wild or in misery to save yourself from the heartache of being misunderstood?

My soul yearned for acceptance and compassion. Maybe yours is too. Being "on" all the time can be grueling. Surveying my past revealed the compassion I gave Hershey far exceeded the compassion and forgiveness I gave myself. I silently cleaned up his messes and replaced anything he might destroy. Yet I constantly reminded myself and others of my own mistakes and destructive behavior.

Somehow, I realized rehearsing his mistakes or threatening his future would be a waste of time. With Hershey, I exercised compassion and learned how to motivate the results I wanted instead of harping on what I saw.

Though hardest on myself, I held others to a high standard as well, and it wasn't just iron sharpening iron. Many times, it was self-righteousness running amok. For example, my habit of bringing up someone's past mistakes to make today's point. Where is the love in that? A habit I fooled myself into thinking was beneficial.

How many times did self-righteous reminders work for me? Did I thank my mother for her motivational speeches that not-so-gently reminded me she told me so? Nope. So why did I believe my reminders were helpful? (By the way, I never caught pneumonia from wearing my cheerleader skirt without sweatpants in the freezing cold).

For me, grace made all the difference. My soul's lack of compassion spewed self-righteousness at me first, before anyone else. I was missing the element of grace which I could only get from time with God. Like Hershey, my training process begins with sit.

The nuggets I picked up from moments of sitting with Him were intertwined with bad habits and lies. To get to the next level, I needed to stay. Take time to meditate on what He taught me previously, even when I couldn't see Him in my current situation. Have the faith that God was with me, never too far, able to protect, and coming back to love on me because of grace.

Then, I needed to *speak*. Not just with words, but allow my life to speak forth the redemptive power of His grace.

For grace to produce fruit in me, I had to see my potential for bad behavior. Defining grace in light of what I had been taught didn't reconcile with what I saw in my life. First, I had to acknowledge that I was judgmental, self-righteous, and prone to lying or compromise to be accepted by others. I had to own up to those traits operating in me, a believer. Only then could I declare that, even with faults and mistakes, there I stood. I was still loved and had an opportunity to do great things for Him and by Him working through me.

Grace became my permission and power to do better, regardless of any residue of my old self. If I had that permission and power, so did the people I judged. In that truth, my soul found the compassion it longed for.

My encouragement to you after my mistakes: resist taking on all the responsibility for a relationship between two people. It's prideful to believe all a relationship needs to survive is you as a chameleon or relational martyr. Some of my relationships never recovered from the resentment of suffocating my true self, then, all of a sudden, changing the game. Once resentment crept in, restoration was nearly impossible.

Once time passed, admitting 'I really didn't like when you did this or that,' highlighted the lie told initially. When a friend said or did something I didn't like, I'd smile through the moment or wouldn't say a word. By the time I mustered up the courage to confess how I really felt as a result of that past incident, it put all other exchanges in question. How often had I faked my responses?

Lies can seem loving, but selfishness or pride generally exist at the root. Love isn't selfish or proud.

I began listening for God's cues. Speaking truth isn't any more selfish than Hershey's gentle reminders that his dinner is late. Keep in mind, Hershey didn't come at me with a barking chorus. He gave me time to hear him and respond accordingly. Don't deliver truth on a trash can lid and expect others to receive it, just because it's truth. Truth isn't watered down by a commitment to deliver it well.

Unhealthy habits can hinder your communication and frustrate what could otherwise be loving relationships. Mine were. My cues came from an animal reflecting what my behavior looked like from the receiver point of view. My realizations stopped me from continuing the crash and burn cycle, yet arrived too late to salvage some friendships. A lesson learned through trial and error is rarely forgotten.

My transition to a new way of living was on trial and only authentic truth could free me. My mission was to un-cover ways to invite others to respect my stance without being self-absorbed. Taking a stand for your needs says you recognize yourself as a gift of God.

For years, I vehemently spoke up for others. God showed me how people connected to my purpose needed me to stand up for my rights as a way of standing for them. My ability to manage uncomfortable interactions communicates what I believe about my purpose. Confi-dence in my purpose suggests to the people in my life that when it counts, I'll stand for them too.

How do you assess your ability to communicate your heart to others? Are you often misinterpreted and misunderstood?

Imagine yourself on a stage. You've been cast as you, and you're rehearsing lines for the coming months. When people pass you on the street and don't return your hello, it doesn't determine whether or not you speak to the next one. You continue following the script. When your lines dictate a hard conversation that's got to occur, it's not optional. Since it's written in the script, you recite the words you've memorized with no thought of responses or emotions you may provoke. You press on realizing that everyone has a part to play.

Newsflash — that's pretty much how life works.

Some days are riddled with drama. Perhaps your soul isn't wounded, but weary. If you decide the pressure is too much, there's no one to replace you. Back out and all the people connected to you, present and future, will miss being exposed to a part of life only you possess. Sound scary? It doesn't have to be.

We aren't meant to live in the shadows of all our past experiences. Life isn't designed to wear us down. Recall a time you spoke up and were teased or berated for your opinion. Now, forget it. Maneuver around that memory and speak. Pain, fear, desire, wisdom, and more require us to take a deep breath and speak.

Yes, when you tried to help your motives were misread. Your words were taken the wrong way. It happened. It's a part of your past. Despite all that, when your neighbor asks what you think, *speak*.

What happened? So you overheard what "they" really think of you. Or, you poured your heart out and it landed on deaf ears and a hard heart. Or worse, on a wagging tongue who spread your secrets. Those experiences don't display what you're entitled to, nor should they write your script. God desires to speak through you and propel you to the center stage of your dreams and desires. When you arrive, you must speak.

There's another side to this coin. Glance backward, to acknowledge anyone hurt by your words. Sincerely ask for forgiveness. Once you do, be released from the situation. Living with a self-imposed muzzle isn't worth your future. Study discretion for the future. Demonstrate that you learned the lesson of your past mistakes by sharing your voice with wisdom and discretion going forward. Be assured, God created each of us for a distinct purpose and isn't put off by our mistakes.

Speak to the fearful child inside you. Reassure and comfort her as you bring her along to see that it gets better.

Speak for those hurt by devastating words, who refuse to open their hearts again.

Speak to your Heavenly Father who isn't surprised when you completely miss the mark. He is willing to clean up all your messes and continue loving you, knowing the likelihood you'll make another mess. Allow His truth to flow through your lips. Make Him a priority. Ask and He'll fill you with wisdom.

*Speak.* Without fear, speak your truth. Don't wait until you suppose that your age, status, or circumstances are worthy of sharing. Or, worthy of others' hearing.

Speak without supposing other opinions are more important because of who they are, or who you're not. Practice sharing your unique insights unapologetically.

I'm so grateful I found my voice and for those who assisted in the process, especially Hershey. It was quite a life change to have "someone" hanging on my every word. The audience isn't always the focus. Sometimes, we just need to practice speaking.

No more living by reciting movie lines and delivering soliloquies. Practice confidence in everyday speech. Exchange communication rather than merely grabbing attention. Gain trust on your way to agreement and healthy relationships. My early years were plagued by my habit of avoiding confrontation because I was afraid of how others would receive what I had to say. My sister Tina flipped that script and showed me that there was fruit in being direct and loving authentically.

I learned to speak a new language because Hershey wasn't afraid to walk right up to me and bark. We communicated head on, fighting through until we finally learned to understand each other.

Speak to the One who isn't afraid to allow you to travel around off leash, despite your prior tendency to go too far. You have plenty to say. And no one can deliver quite like you.

### Soul Training Tips

- Don't respond to past hurt using your present conversations.
- Grace gives us the permission and power to do better, regardless of old behaviors.
- Your future is too important to live with a self-imposed muzzle.
- Truth isn't watered down by your commitment to deliver it well.
- Speak with the confidence of knowing you're in God, and He's in you.

# 5 | LEAVE IT

Right out of college, I spent some time working at a clothing store. I liked the flexibility, the discount, and the break it gave my brain. Folding sweaters is a far cry from neuroscience, so I welcomed the break.

Several weeks in, a coworker disappeared. Fired for stealing.

I was in shock. She didn't really seem the type. Turns out, she would look the other way while her friend hid items she took into the fitting room to smuggle them out of the store.

Stealing never appealed to me. Not a friend in the world could convince me that 'we won't get caught.' The idea of being arrested and prosecuted was a sufficient deterrent. The thought of them calling my mother worked even better.

Unfortunately, I wasn't as immune to other vices and

bad habits.

In my lifetime, I've driven too fast, drank, lied, cheated, and cursed until new habits edged out those tendencies. Once the old tendencies lost their appeal, it became easy to walk away and not look back. (Except, maybe, for the fast driving. Moving to Florida changed that one.)

Despite my former vices, I don't understand the draw toward activities that could end my life or take away my freedom. We hear news stories about thieves and reckless or drunk drivers almost daily. Each probably believed they wouldn't be caught or hurt. Why weren't the potential consequences weren't enough of a deterrent to affect their behavior?

We all have different input influencing our decisions. Ultimately, my self-control dictates how I respond to temptation and separates me from those who end up on the news. What's one of self-control's biggest enemies? What I feel I deserve. Ask me why I continue to snack on French fries, chips, and popcorn when I'm watching my weight. My likely response is, 'Well, I've been working hard all week. I *deserved* it.'

Similarly, there are self-entitled folks come to believe their desire is sufficient impetus to take what they want. The desire to possess plus feelings of entitlement override self-control. When I want tortilla chips, offering me carrot sticks is futile when I feel I'm entitled to what I want. Making a new choice required training myself away from entitlement. Diminishing its appeal. Choking entitlement until it gave way to reason.

I had to begin to learn ways to process the difference between desire and what's best. My waistline cried out for me to make greater efforts at learning to practice self-control and tell myself no.

With dogs, we tell them to *'leave it.'*

Like any dog with a nose, Hershey is drawn to smelly things — good or bad, alive or dead. He's as likely to chase a live squirrel as to walk up and sniff a dead one.

Early one winter morning, we walked along the edges of a nearby golf course just after the snow melted. I kept him on a long leash, so I had to constantly navigate the trees to keep him from getting tangled. Oblivious to my efforts, Hershey forged ahead with his nose to the ground.

We walked along; frozen leaves and snow crunched under my feet while Hershey moved around silently and stealthily. When he stopped abruptly, I didn't realize he wasn't moving, so I kept walking, which nearly cost me a pair of boots. When I finally looked to see what had his nose, it was a dead squirrel. One more step and those boots would've been trash. Though the squirrel looked to be frozen solid and probably wouldn't have oozed, that walk home would've been those boots' last dance on my feet. The look on your face now is likely the same one

Hershey gave as I shrieked, yanking him away. I may have managed to say, "Leave it." I forget due to the trauma.

The command to "leave it" most resembles a basic "no" used, for instance, when a child reaches toward a hot stove or wanders near the stairs. It's often stern and meant to stop the pup in his tracks. Since dogs tend to lead with their noses, the command requires a high level of devotion to pull them away from stinky treasures. Dogs have millions more smell receptors than humans, so easily distracted is a gross understatement for them.

In training "leave it," I encouraged Hershey's sense of reward using treats. Yummy treats that he could smell from a distance were the high-value reward. To increase payoff, I used a different treat or toy as the training item.

First, I put the training treat in my palm and placed my hand in front of his face. I gave him the freedom to take it from my palm every time. Easy. After repeating that once or twice, I put the training treat near his nose, but closed my fist as he leaned in.

"Leave it!" I yelled.

Clearly confused, he licked and nibbled at my hand trying to get it open.

Once he gave up and sat down, I would calmly repeat, "Leave it," and present the reward from my other hand. In time, he began to exercise momentary self-control, trusting there was something better in store. Each time Hershey controlled his urge to challenge or disobey the command, he earned the high-value reward. Whoever designed positive reinforcement training is a genius!

Using positive reinforcement, Hershey began to leverage the rules. Remember learning to multiply? In the beginning, it was straightforward. You could memorize your 'times tables' and be successful without really understanding the rules. As the problems got more advanced, rules governed how we solved for the answers. To do well, we also needed a good grasp on previous rules. Multiplication is easier once you know how to add and carry values, right?

Same with training. Rules build on each other. However, managing some rules well doesn't guarantee a better response to temptation around other rules. Based on our training though, Hershey's behavior shift progressed smoothly. He fought to overcome urges around his sense of smell and insatiable appetite. Consistent rewards encouraged his continued obedience.

Unfortunately in my own journey, my strong sense of rejection pulled me toward interim fixes. My insecurities whispered lies to me. Having to wait made the lies seem true, so I stuck my nose where it didn't belong. Where Hershey let his trust in a future reward guide him, I engaged in back-up plans that held me back.

I needed to learn the rules on how to trust God and

the people He placed in my life. I needed to build on those rules and understand that past rejection didn't entitle me to present mistrust. When I allowed impatience and old thought patterns to creep in, I postponed my rewards. Hershey's simplistic obedience demonstrated a better way to submit to God instead of thinking I knew best. An example of what that looked like? Trusting that whatever and whomever I willingly released made room for better.

Why wasn't that already a part of my life as a believer? Because again, I managed my relationship with God as if He were man. Judging Him by man's responses to me in the areas of faithfulness, consistency, and love justified my doubt. At that time, I had no experience in unconditional faith. Rather than trust in a future reward, I went with what I could see.

I lived that way for years, exercising a "head" faith which said, 'He can do the impossible. I just may not qualify.' While serving and teaching others about the real thing, I routinely practiced works-based faith. Ignorant to my hypocrisy, I continued trying to control my surroundings…until my second husband and I separated.

One Wednesday night, I was teaching a discipleship class at my church based on the book of Romans when it suddenly hit me. My breath caught and my chest clenched at the realization: I was living by works and not faith.

I wasn't living the very things I taught others as truth.

I truly believed in a faithful God who would do what He promised in His word. However, over the years I became increasingly skeptical about whether He would do it for me. I deemed myself unworthy of certain answers. Like a coward, I decided I wasn't worth what God already said was mine to have. That day, my hypocrisy caught in my throat with my words and tears burned my eyes.

Instead of maneuvering around it, I chose to use it as a teaching moment. I confessed. After all, discipleship isn't just about the biblical principles; it's also about life on life experiences. When certain prayers, namely those around marriage and family issues from youth to adulthood, didn't turn out the way I hoped and prayed, I made a justification, which grew into a works-based faith. That is the reason I pretended everything was okay and hesitated to pray big prayers and ask God to reconcile my marriage.

Before that day, my students had no idea I was separated or going through anything at all. The discipleship program was new and I didn't know anyone in this, my first class. We were only a few weeks into classes and I was hiding behind my platinum ring with the princess cut stone and my mask, as usual. Sharing my truth sparked conversations that deeply bonded our group from that day.

Identifying the foundation for my lack of faith was easy. Basically, I wanted control over the outcome of my circumstances. I wasn't acquainted with the love in "no," so I concluded I didn't qualify for my request. I mean, why else wouldn't God answer my prayer to save my marriage? Surely, He wasn't asking me to "leave it." In retrospect, it wasn't the act He commanded of me; it was the trust.

Instead of relinquishing control and trusting Him for the steps to repair the brokenness, I furiously tried to fix things on my own. When my efforts failed, I reverted to the idea that I irreparably damaged the relationship and God could no longer fix it. How's that for pride!

Pride wasn't the only issue. Residue of disappointment over the years, including a previous divorce, affected how I dealt with people. Disappointment tainted my belief system, so I wanted to feel I had a hand in any negative outcomes. Make it my fault rather than God's. Deep down, I knew I couldn't afford to allow disappointment from unanswered prayer to harden my heart toward God. So, I battled to keep my beliefs about faith separate from how I felt about my life circumstances.

Let that sink in for a moment. I wanted to control how my lack of faith affected my relationship with God. Major problem.

Turns out, training Hershey was a great outlet for my control issues. Early on when he was in puppy preschool, we learned a new command each week and were responsible to practice the commands outside of class. My competitive nature practiced with him diligently each week. Although I trained him, in the end it was up to him. On one hand, I wanted to curb his behavior at home and in public. On the other, I was prepping for graduation and the final exam. I wanted to win.

On final exam day in puppy preschool, all the puppies and their families sat in a large circle for the test. The trainer called out each command and watched for our raised arm signaling which dog finished first. At the end, she tallied all the points to crown the valedictorian.

I knew Hershey would excel in most of the commands, but held concern about his ability to "leave it" with the pressure on. Remarkably, as soon as Hershey heard the stern, "Leave it!," he darted clear across the room. Embarrassed? For sure. Trainer Debbie may have felt my pain. She said sweetly, "If your dog runs away to avoid temptation, that's just fine. They still get the point."

Ha.

Never mind my puppy had to be recalled from the other side of the room to resume the test. We sailed through those commands! Hershey tied with a standard poodle for valedictorian that day. Accomplishment washed over me. My pup was well trained and fairly balanced. The days I got it wrong, yelled too loudly, and punished too harshly hadn't stunted his growth. At the trainer's suggestion, Hershey and I continued to practice and reinforce his commands long after preschool ended.

A few years later, an attack by another dog left Hershey skittish and overly protective. Hershey and his dog walker were getting off the elevator when another dog, Jade, and her walker were getting on. Though Jade was known to be aggressive, her less experienced substitute dog walker didn't know to avoid tight spaces with other dogs.

Days before Hershey, Jade had attacked a small pug, leaving him badly injured. Then Hershey ended up with a long scratch on his face. Even worse, after the attack, the mere sight of another dog set off fireworks in his brain. Our walks became stressful to the point of tears. (Mine). The trauma of that attack left Hershey defensive. He growled and lunged forward with the strength of an ox. Similar to the time after his skirmish with Charlie, we had to avoid close contact with other dogs until his confidence returned.

For weeks, our walks became training sessions again. I vigilantly looked out for dogs approaching. Upon spotting one, I worked on controlling the environment.

*"Sit."*

*"Stay."*

Then I held a treat near Hershey's nose as the dog passed. *"Leave it."*

If Hershey held his peace, reward. If he growled or, God forbid, lunged, I put the treat away. *"Bad boy."*

Day after day, we worked to restore trust that not every dog was out to get us. After a few weeks, a dog could pass us without incident using treats and sit. Weeks later, we could pass other dogs without stopping. Success!

Until we reached that point, doggy friends from the park and their owners seemed sad at having to keep their distance during Hershey's recovery. One day, they were friends. The next, no more. When I explained the reason behind Hershey's outbursts, the other dog owners didn't seem hopeful. Though I cried frustrated tears at his drastic change in temperament, I never doubted that my training investment would pay off.

Hershey needed time and space and someone patient enough to walk with him through the hard days and celebrate with him in the good ones. I owed him that and more. Moreover, I had to see that I needed the same. My normal preference was to walk through difficult times alone and not bring anyone along with me.

With all I endured, what made me think I could remain in the same environment as my trauma and be healed all on my own? Two factors supported that thinking. First, my inability to acknowledge the depth of my pain. Secondly, pride and shame suggested that I shoulder the responsibility of repentance and soul transformation alone.

Good friends asked how I was doing.

*"I'm good."*

The ones who could see behind my mask replied, *"No. No, you're not."*

I would shake off their inquiries and put on a quick show to change the subject. Most times, they backed down and left me to my inner drama.

Why go through those antics? Because insecurity is tricky and switches back and forth between 'you got this' and 'you're not worthy' without warning. Since my insecurity lay buried under feelings of rejection, offset by charm and wit, I gained and lost friends with ease. Though I held on desperately, some of my favorite relationships imploded. In the ashes, my soul screamed at me for help as an old thought resurfaced: *I'm not worth fighting for.*

I liken it to the feeling I get when I find out one of my favorite shows is ending. The betrayal of it all! Though I was faithful week after week, someone decided the program was no longer worthy of its time slot. So, they yank it. Without asking. (The nerve)! Sometimes, the end is abrupt, leaving storylines frayed with unanswered questions. Letter campaigns for another season may work, but usually I'm forced to adjust my viewing habits. Find alternatives to replace what is no more.

I also think about the actors in those roles. The joy of having signed a contract wanes because a decision out of their control leaves them available once again. Time to dust off those headshots and set up some auditions. Now transfer that analogy to me. When life shifts, it's time to dust off my resumé. Here I am again, auditioning for a role in someone's life.

Regrettably, since I can't control other people, I don't always get to choose when my contract is over. When relationships end, the timing's often inconvenient and abrupt. Loose ends remain. And even when new people fill the time slots, it's sad when I can't explain why some of my favorites disappeared.

When Hershey went from eating treats from my hand to being on the receiving end of yelling and a closed fist, it must have been pretty confusing. His initial reaction was to try and get my hand open. As a result of trial, error and training, he put the experiences together and changed his approach. His reward was immediate.

Why wasn't I as astute as my dog?

Because initially I wasn't engaged with anyone to help me see me. Trying to extract lessons from daily life on my own and get my issues healed at the same time played out like someone going to physical therapy while in a body cast. As healing came and seeped into my soul, I began to itch and sweat inside my body cast. I poked holes in my cast. Or in other words, I was closed off and only interacted with people in small doses.

When I began to open up again, I saw how the mistrust I created in my dark moments kept some people at a distance. There were several who didn't want to give me another try. Loss stepped in again as my teacher. I couldn't blame them. Be that as it may, their stance confirmed it: I really *wasn't* worth fighting for.

During that time, I wasn't fit to heal, sharpen, restore, or reconcile. On the path back to wholeness, I'll always be grateful for the friends who came through the process with me. And I hold no grudge against those who didn't. We all have a journey we must travel.

Every chance I got, I asked for forgiveness. Broken inside, I was like a driver who fell asleep at the wheel. Not malicious, yet still destructive and potentially deadly. Changing meant getting out of the driver's seat.

For a while, Hershey remained a large part of my reason for living. Though I understood God's love for me, I had reached a crossroad where I couldn't go further without loving myself. It was time to leave behind the idea that everyone else had worth except me. It was time to shed a persona who resembled me, yet nobody seemed to recognize. Set it aside to find the real me.

In other words, *leave it.*

Hershey participated in my journey to loving myself in ways no human could at that time. I didn't share negative self-talk with him. Hershey didn't have the language or capacity to allow me to rationalize away my worth. He also didn't think to treat me any differently at 245 pounds than he did at 200 pounds. (If he had, maybe I'd have lost weight for him, too)!

There was no criticism or condemnation from him about what I didn't finish or did incorrectly. His affection existed in the moment. He was completely present and expected me to reciprocate. Whether he needed food, water, a walk, or for me to lift one end of the couch so he could retrieve his toy, Hershey's gratitude was consistent. When I messed up, he quickly shifted from sad eyes to doggy kisses. Over time, he helped me escape the negativity I levied at myself for failures I caused.

The biggest hurdle I crossed with God's prompting and Hershey's help was abandoning the lifeless depression I cradled for months on end. I desperately needed to just leave it.

One day, I was in the restroom going through my morning routine when in my heart I heard the question, *'When will you stop just existing and start **living** again?'* Initially, I was too deep in denial to immediately process the words. I wasn't prepared to be honest. Who could I tell that while teaching on faith and trusting God in our discipleship gatherings, some days I had to negotiate taking a shower and brushing my teeth? On the days I didn't have to leave home other than to walk Hershey, my existence only required food, water, and breathing.

Looking back, my behavior seems an obvious depiction of being depressed. Being able to "turn it on" when necessary fooled me into thinking I was okay. Since Hershey was silent on the matter, it wasn't until my other therapist, the one with the PhD, clued me in that I had to face it — I was depressed. She insisted it wasn't normal to work from home 8-10 hours per day and feel a need to spend any free time with my dog. Whenever I did venture out, I ended up rushing home to him as soon as possible. After being gone for more than a few hours I became anxious to get back. I didn't simply relish being away from people; I felt compelled toward it.

The hypocrisy my life had become seriously endangered my walk with God. He sent messages of "leave it" through His Word and other people. When I didn't immediately obey, I experienced a sharp decline in my ability to hear and obey His other commands.

My actions showed that I feared disappointing people more than I feared disappointing God. I hid my brokenness from people when I never could hide it from Him. Many of my disciplines remained in place, but my discernment and boundaries suffered. Even as I pulled away from long-time friends and the fellowship we usually shared, I remained hopeful they would pick up on what was happening. I convinced myself that I would respond if they came to my emotional rescue. When they didn't come, I ran toward getting comfort from other people who also couldn't see what was really happening to me.

The message that I wasn't worth fighting for continued to rage.

All along I missed the big picture. God desired me to be the one to "leave it" and turn to Him. It wasn't in His plan for some Superman or Superwoman to pull me out of the pit I was in. Anger and frustration did nothing to change my situation. Full restoration came when I finally decided to embrace the lifeline of grace that would keep me connected to Him.

The idea that God loved me fiercely, even when I wasn't on top of all my "works," began my grace journey back to Him. In that journey, prayer, rejecting negative self-talk and thought patterns, along with being brutally honest about my progress helped restore my worth in my heart. Finally, I began responding to training.

Hershey's role in my leaving the shores of depression was as instrumental to my restoration as my encounter with God's grace. Sometimes his presence alone, curled up in the bend of my knee as I lay on the couch, brought comfort. Other times, seeing him romp around and play inspired me to work toward adopting an unrestrained, carefree attitude. God's grace empowered me to travel the path to that freedom.

My human therapist was instrumental in a different way. Initially, I only decided to visit her to talk through my second divorce which seemed inevitable at the time. When she asked why I was there, I literally said I wanted to deal with my feelings about this divorce so I wouldn't break down in the courtroom. In her humanity and expertise, she did what Hershey couldn't. She saw through my request and compelled me to want more. A Christian therapist, she refused to allow me to be half-healed from the issues at the root of my behaviors. She also insisted I go beyond a surface, head-driven relationship with God and His Word.

In these years, I also had a close relationship with one of the pastors at my church. Together with my therapist, she refueled my ability to trust that God wasn't indifferent about me. From them I learned to embrace the fact that He wholly loves me and is completely invested in me.

Immune to my masks and religious rationalizations, these two taught me how to reshape my trust and walk out vulnerability. They saw me on the edge of transparency, rarely becoming vulnerable. They pointed out the ways I opened up to let people see me, but made sure they weren't allowed to touch.

Once I learned to identify people who were equipped to touch and help heal my wounds, my healing was underway. As I discovered that certain behaviors didn't fit with my new mindset, my wholeness journey began.

By getting help, I finally reached the next level of soul training: leaving behind my quest to do it all on my own.

No more flying solo with me and Hershey against the world. To positively affect my relationships with people, I had to submit part of the process to people!

Why have people journey with you? Because feeling lonely or void can stir you to compromise and to revert to old, raggedy standards and boundaries. When I compromised, I lowered my defenses and gave permission for the wrong folks to come close. In lonely moments, it slipped my mind that only God could fill some voids. I fell flat on my face. Or on my back. More than once. Once guilt joined the emptiness inside, a snowball effect began. So, I needed someone privy to my habits and weaknesses to keep better options at the forefront of my mind and help guide my decisions.

Decision making is one step toward change; gauging progress is another. Without the benefit of other people, I could trick myself into believing I was doing better and going deeper than I really was. Being open to evaluation kept me honest. In time, although my heart was breaking into pieces because of divorce, I was feeling lighter than ever because I could finally see the core of what had been troubling me.

Running came easy for me, but it didn't accomplish anything. A healthy soul required me to press in, not settling for the outskirts of deliverance and wholeness. The foundation of mistrust I built because of my inability to love and trust myself had to be destroyed. My core beliefs had to include that I am a human representation of God's image, seated in heavenly places with Him.

Is God trying to get a new set of core beliefs to you? Are there habits and mindsets He wants you to leave behind? Do you have the right person(s) walking you through your life-changing decisions? Take a moment to ask God how to navigate around what's trying to destroy you. Allow Him to point out who and what goes with you, and what you should leave behind. In some instances the idea of leaving may bring pain, but you could be destroyed if you stay. *Leave it.*

When you think that a bag of chips, a whole pizza, or hunk of cake will make it all better, *leave it.* (I may or may not have tried this a time or two).

Any ideas you have about quitting the process of your transformation, *leave it.*

Know that depression is a force you'll need help defeating. Stop rolling over it as if it doesn't exist. *Sit.*

Stop running from place to place, trying to find someone to fix you. *Stay.*

Be vulnerable with someone who's equipped to handle you and what's attacking you. *Speak.*

Whether or not you initially see the problem and even if you don't agree, walk away from the waves of comfortable chaos. Just *leave it.*

Leave tendencies of suspicion and mistrust.

Leave the picture you painted with your expectations.

Reject the tendency to look at roles others played in your disappointments. We possess full control over our actions. Looking at what someone else did or didn't do keeps the merry-go-round of regret spinning, and we get sicker and sicker. It's time to get off!

Stop looking in the broken mirror of your past self and live in your today. Push beyond simply existing and determine who you will become, irrespective of who and where you are today. What is God saying about your future? You can't hear His plans when your ears are filled with your voice singing the blues.

Leave the crowds for a moment and allow your Trainer to whisper to you about possibilities and promises you have yet to tap into. You may be facing a dire situation, but that doesn't mean your best days are behind you. Redefine your future with renewed focus.

### *Soul Training Tips*

- Past rejection doesn't entitle you to present mistrust.
- Trust that whatever you willingly release makes room for better.
- Disobedience in one area causes a sharp decline in our

ability to discern and hear God in other areas.

- God desires for you to "leave it" and turn to Him as an act of your will.
- Walk away from comfortable chaos and seek God in order to redefine your future.

# 6 | FETCH

One of my favorite things about the way Hershey and I play these days is how well he understands the rules. Our early days of fetch resembled a circus act, and I was the clown. (Don't judge me. Fetch is harder than it looks)!

I throw the ball. *Check.*

Dog chases ball. *Check.*

Dog brings ball back and drops it to be thrown again. *Check.*

No, really. Check and see which way my dog went.

With the ball in his mouth, Hershey would come charging in my direction then run right past me. I think many times he and I played different games.

Fetch, like other games we play with our pets, is designed to tire our good buddies out. Also, the time we spend with them increases the bond, similar to taking them for walks. Learning to fetch requires focus, engagement, and exchange. The objective is for pups to complete the entire sequence: fetch, grab, bring, and drop. Take it from me, those frisbee playing dog-human teams make it look easier than it is.

I tried adding helpful instructions like, "Go get it," which he did.

I followed up with a sing-song voice, "Bring it to Momma," as sweetly as I could muster. No dice. Ran past me like a raging bull. Head down, ball in teeth, flying right by me.

I wish I could say I never got impatient, but I did. Better results? Nah. Angry responses simply reinforced his resolve. Hershey certainly didn't rush to bring a beloved ball back to a crazy lady yelling in his direction. For the most part, though, we still had a good time. Mostly because I got smart and brought an extra squeaky toy and treats to help the game along when we got stuck.

Thankfully, Hershey grasped the concept in time. One night, our lives depended on it.

I didn't take Hershey to many dog parks because I wasn't good at watching him wrestle with other dogs. Plus, since other dogs didn't take kindly to him playing fetch with their balls, we got into scrapes. To keep the peace, I either had to carry bags of treats to bribe the other dogs, or we'd visit parks at off-hours.

One night, a few weeks after we moved to a new

apartment, Hershey and I visited a park in the area. This park was wide open without the internal and external gates to help introduce a dog slowly to other dogs and discourage non-dog people from cutting through. Most people let their dogs run free, despite having little control or recall. I longed to see my pup run free, but generally left him on a leash unless we were there alone.

This night, I surveyed the park and didn't see anyone, so I let Hershey loose. He ran around like a wild man. Suddenly, he stopped, ears perked toward heaven.

I failed to be vigilant and was about to pay.

A man was cutting through the park on his phone. He was distracted, talking loudly. I didn't have time to grab Hershey before he took off like lightning toward the voice. I knew calling him was futile, so I tried warning the man.

"Excuse me! That's my dog! He's friendlyyyyyyyyy!" I kept yelling. The man was too involved in his call to hear me. Finally, he saw Hershey and started screaming.

Let me interject a disclaimer. When I relayed this story right after it happened, I wanted some reassurance that my feelings were valid. Shaken, I relayed the highlights through sobs and broken sentences. The person I called said, "I don't blame him. Lisa, you're the only one who looks at Hershey and sees 'baby.' Everyone else sees 'big dog.'"

Not helpful.

Perhaps I should've understood or been able to see things from the man's point of view. I couldn't in the moment, and feel the same today.

Panting, I arrived at the screaming man seconds after Hershey, who, by the way, was oblivious to the commotion. Worse, he didn't realize the man's fear. Fully panicked, the man repeatedly swung his messenger bag at Hershey, who was having the time of his life running circles around him. The man was yelling while Hershey barked back at him like, 'This is the best game ever!'

I added to the confusion, screaming, "Please stop yelling so he can hear me!"

Repeatedly, the man said, "You better get him!" I responded by really trying to get Hershey. The three of us did a dance for what seemed like ages.

In the melee, the man pulled a knife from his coat, started slashing at the space between him and Hershey, and yelled, "I'm gonna kill him!"

All rational thinking left me. I jumped in front of the knife, shaking as I calmly declared, "No, you're not." Then, fear took over, and I hollered, "Now, SHUT UP!"

Apparently, when the man reached in his coat to grab his knife, he took his glove off. Because as he swung, a glove fell to the ground.

Hershey, oblivious to any danger, figured this was a new element of the game. Without me saying a word, he snatched the glove and took off running.

Immediately, I shifted into a shaky, sing-song voice, saying "Bring it to Momma" while digging for a treat. Curious for the reward, Hershey came over, dropped the glove at my feet, and sat down. I grabbed his collar, hooked his leash, and gave him the treat.

"You're gonna give him a _____ treat after that?!"

"Yes! I told you to stop yelling so he could hear me. He's a puppy!"

"That's no _____ puppy! You better be glad you got him, 'cause I was gonna kill him."

I don't know if the man ever heard my, "No you weren't," as he resumed his call, littered with plenty of profanity as he told his friend, 'I was just trying to get to church and this _____ dog came out of nowhere.'

Full disclosure, I wrote down the man's license plate and looked for him for weeks and didn't even know why. He had no clue that it all could've gone much worse. What if Hershey didn't know how to play fetch! I don't know whether Hershey's response to me saved the day, or if the glove fell at just the right time. Whichever it was, I was thrilled we escaped safely.

Even more exciting was the way Hershey brought me the glove rather than doing his raging bull routine. Retrieving the ball, or in this case the glove, could mean the end of the game, a sad time for him. When he returned the item, he wasn't sure if it was the end - the last throw. The uncertainty usually made him tentative, which frustrated me. In this instance, he didn't hesitate. Score!

After playing fetch with Hershey for a while, I learned the underlying issue influencing the way he played with me was trust. The probability of him dropping the ball at my feet to continue the game depended upon whether he believed I would throw it again. As a puppy, his primary needs were food and play. So, his running away with the ball was an effort to control the game and prolong his feelings of satisfaction. Unfortunately, control was a strategy I knew well. Like Hershey, I just didn't realize how often I was using it.

A few years ago, my therapist described how she viewed my relationship habits. She said I'd open my arms, waving enthusiastically, calling people in my direction. Once they got close, I'd fold my arms saying, in effect, 'Nah, I was just kidding.' Her accuracy prevented me from getting angry at how rude I came off in that description. In my game of dysfunctional fetch, I controlled the dynamics of the game and whether I let anyone else play or took my ball and went home.

The more Hershey matured, the more he brought the ball back to me. However, getting him to drop it was a different story. That was the next level in our relationship. He would come close, then let my behavior dictate the next phase of the game. He wouldn't drop the ball at all, or he'd drop it and hover over it. When I reached in, he snatched it away. For a while, I would fight the ball out of his mouth. Later, I started exchanging the ball for a treat, incorporating a high value exchange to build his trust.

Our methods were different, but our objectives similar: keep the fun going. The lengths I went to in order to avoid pain demonstrated how far out of character my soul cravings could take me. My need for soul training grew out of the emotional crutches I built specifically to help me navigate rejection. Rejection was my biggest enemy aside from fear; I believed if I kept the fun going, I could keep rejection at bay.

Ever heard the saying, 'what you focus on becomes bigger?' By focusing on how to avoid rejection, I developed a relationship with it. I consulted rejection before I made a phone call, went on a date, and even before I went to church. Rejection influenced my decisions and perpetuated unhealthy behavior cycles. Either I acted out to "cause" the rejection or attempted to control the environment and avoid it. Like Hershey, I wanted to keep playing for as long as possible.

As with most of us, Hershey's endless need to play gave way to maturity, and further, trust. Somehow, he had confidence that even if the game ended, we would play again. Or, we'd do something else fun. My trainer pup laid out another exercise sequence for me to use in my relationships. Trust.

In my world, new friends often had to bow to the suspicion an old friend created. Same with men. I engaged quickly, but not deeply. I threw out information long before I was sure new friends cared to know or could handle what I was sharing. Then, if they didn't come back with what I wanted or needed from the relationship, I closed the window of trust. Lucky for me, in our training relationship Hershey modeled what developing real trust looked like in practice. First, I had to surrender my heart to the One who had been trying to engage me for years.

God desires that we allow Him to be the gatekeeper of our hearts. I tossed my heart away to different people, some of whom weren't even paying attention. Then I waited, secretly hoping to get it back one day in the same condition. How ironic that I doubted my worth, yet held tight to the most valuable part of me? No part of me was equipped to guard my heart well.

Where Proverbs 4:23[2] dictates that we guard our hearts diligently, we go wrong thinking that we can do it in our strength. Hershey's carefree attitude and quick forgiveness demonstrated to me how bound I was! I guarded my heart by running around putting up walls trying to prevent

---

[2] *Watch over your heart with all diligence, for from it flow the springs of life.*
*Proverbs 4:23 New American Standard Bible*

the wrong people from getting in. They always did because I was too tired from my efforts to be an effective watchman.

When Hershey evaded me in some of our games, like running away during fetch, he never managed to alienate me with his antics. After all, he just wanted to keep playing. Meanwhile, I walked through life simultaneously afraid to play the game and afraid not to. Obviously fearful of being rejected, but unwilling to wait on the sideline and chance not getting picked.

I was missing out; not really living.

Part of the reason Hershey couldn't alienate me was because of how much I loved him and genuinely wanted to give him what he wanted and needed. Why couldn't I see that's exactly what my Father wanted for me? Part of me believed God wouldn't fail me. A larger part didn't want to take the chance and be wrong. I knew I couldn't sustain being without Him, yet I kept Him at a distance in an effort to prevent the unbearable. In the ways I quit on myself and others quit on me, maybe He would too.

My philosophy seemed to suggest I go "fetch" the love God had thrown into the earth for me, which was a lie. He didn't throw anything. He brought love to the door of my heart, patiently waiting for me to open up and participate in an exchange with Him. Not only didn't I bring love back to Him, I didn't even lavish it on myself.

For the record, having a tug-of-war contest with God is no fun. Believing that you know better than He what's best for you is an invitation to sleepless nights. In my push and pull, I continued engaging Him the best way I knew how. I loved conversing with Him via the scriptures, so I memorized and meditated on scripture frequently. While the scriptures lived in me, they weren't showing up in my actions. Scripture couldn't live through me as long as I remained broken and mistrusted God over the times things didn't go my way.

Over the years, I watched God restore marriages all around me. I made it a personal project to reconcile my unanswered prayer in my heart and not get angry at God. How? By resolving that the failure was in me, something I did or hadn't done.

Walking away from God over the offense of my unmet expectations wasn't an option. Even in the face of divorce, I refused to allow marriage failure to sour me on God's faithfulness. Determined to shield my heart and keep a level of faith, I chose to believe "lightly." Diet faith. A lighter version of the real thing, with some ingredients being watered down substitutes.

It seems completely odd now that I thought I loved God for years when I really didn't trust Him. I mistook a crisis of faith for mere disappointment. I painted a picture that He was playing favorites and I didn't make the cut.

The raw truth: I couldn't distinguish between what He offered me and what others threw out and I picked up.

Each time this thought surfaced and I chose to believe God answers everyone else's prayers over mine, I called Him a liar. Though my brain perceived the bold lie at the root of my thinking, my pain perpetuated it throughout my soul. It was up to me to wrestle with the lie until the truth of who God is and who He is to me reemerged in my soul and in my life.

For me to move beyond my ideas that God would disappoint me, I had to stop using people as a frame of reference for Him. Even harder, I had to resolve once and for all that I was worthy of His love and faithfulness. As I moved into a relationship of trust with Him, God began to show me the unhealthy ways I presented myself to the world. I was terrible at fetch in real life!

Imagine if you thought you were playing tennis, even though you kept serving over and over without allowing the other person to engage. No matter how many times people tried to coach you or reacquaint you with the rules, you kept serving and serving and serving. That was me.

In relationship, I was neither expecting nor preparing to receive anything in return. I grew tired while my serves became more and more wild. Why keep going? I never saw myself being engaged in the volley. I wasn't convinced that I'd know how to return if someone were interested enough to hit the ball to me. I had to learn how to receive, but I also had to learn how to wait to see if I should be chasing what was hit in my direction!

As my four-legged trainer opened my heart to the benefits of the volley, I began to slow down in my pursuit of people and do some self-examination. Rather than serving into an abyss, not really knowing who was on the other side of the net, I grew more intentional. I slowed down and paid attention to my surroundings. Once I aimed with purpose, the trajectory of my life changed. This wasn't an outward change as much as an inward one. My "no" became as important as my "yes," and my life satisfaction went through the roof.

Having struggled with depression off and on for years, the new place of joy that didn't depend on others was a fresh, soothing balm to my soul. If I had any regrets it would be that in those years I fueled my depression and suppressed the authentic me, I hurt others.

In my twenties, I foolishly flirted a lot while driving. A few times, I pulled over! (I know, right?!) One day, I met a guy we'll call Jared. He was handsome, kind, and hardworking. I ended up being crazy about him, and he me. He drove miles to come to my apartment, but I was a terrible hostess in my living space and heart space. I had no clue how to receive him or his heart.

I remember visiting his family once, and his mother

was very open about how much she disliked me. I didn't understand it then, but I believe she saw what I couldn't — a young lady who didn't know who she was and wouldn't be able to navigate and take care of her son's tender heart and feelings. After meeting her, I subconsciously agreed with her assessment that he was too good for me, and true to form, I completely ruined our relationship. This time, there was no relief in running away. I regretted the way I treated Jared and for years wondered, 'What if?'

The hardest part about my failed attempts at life's game of fetch and my depression-driven mishaps are people like Jared who I hurt. Weaved throughout my story are tales of pain, but in some of those stories, I was the one holding the knife. True maturity is realizing that you've been more than a victim; sometimes, you were the perpetrator.

Being slow to understand our impact on the world is dangerous. We need help pointing out our problem areas. Many of us missed out on emotional development lessons because as teens we got most of our advice from peers. Then, as adults, we try to put the pieces back together.

I've done my best to ask for forgiveness and change my behavior so I'm not a repeat offender. Continuing to live the adage that "hurt people hurt people" as the offender wasn't my desire. Managing my soul and employing healthy relational habits was key to my moving away from perpetrator and victim roles. Before I ever stepped foot inside a therapist's office, Hershey trained me to look at my mannerisms. As I observed how I caught whatever I was thrown and gave love in such a lopsided manner, I began adapting to a new way of being. Then my true self, with all her misguided methods, started coming into view.

Bottom line, God used Hershey to help train me to trust the exchange. I saw how I could be nurturing without being overindulgent. No more tossing out favors, gifts, and compliments to see who sticks. Having honest interactions with friends helped me manage my emotional risk. I grew to embrace the benefits of vulnerability more than avoiding the risks of it.

Who is God aligning you with to help you expand your practice of self-care in new ways? Do you take care of your emotions and protect your soul from predatory people? How often are you checking in with your loved ones to get feedback on what they're receiving from you?

If you are running from love that's being tossed in your direction, perhaps it's time you sit back and evaluate. Instead of fetch, maybe a baseball approach would work better in your life.

When a pitcher fires the ball at a batter, the batter doesn't swing at every ball that comes in his direction. He's evaluating the pitches as they come to decide when to swing. If he chooses not to swing at a "perfect" pitch, there's an umpire there to correct his view. God is our Umpire. He's standing behind us, hoping that we use our life experiences to evaluate when to swing.

Once we connect with the right pitch, God has the Holy Spirit positioned at first base to coach you on your run. After the initial connection, it's all about following the Leader and getting home. As you get closer to home, you'll likely encounter an encourager at third base to remind you of your ability to do all things. In the end, you win!

The One who never lost a battle wants to engage with you to strengthen you and guarantee your victory.

Part of my problem in relationships was I didn't seem to be reading from the same playbook as everyone else. Sometimes, I didn't seem to be playing the same game! While it was painful to be benched until my skills matched the league I'm in, I am the better for it.

Do you need some time on the bench?

Or a refresher course on the playbook?

As you reach for higher heights in life and love, my hope is that you see your worth and not just your want. Hershey's presence highlighted the ways my self-care fell short and didn't match his care. I kept attempting to love people in ways that were basically foreign because I hadn't practiced loving myself, which is why I wasn't getting results from the things I tossed out. Self-care provides opportunities to practice loving ourselves so we know what it looks and feels like.

Are you making efforts to improve your self-care? Look at the ways you engage with yourself. How is your self-talk? Do you make effort to work on the things about yourself that you say you don't like? Or do you constantly berate yourself about what you can't seem to change? Do you make time for what you find fun or relaxing, or are you living an 'all work and no play' lifestyle?

Without an element of self-care, or soul-care, the energy you expend on loving someone else may end up like my early games of fetch with Hershey. You will keep tossing and tossing, without enjoying the benefit of having someone bring it back to you. With the right focus, you'll move from fetch to baseball, getting a chance to pitch and take turns at bat.

Are you ready to commit to training camp?

### *Soul Training Tips*

- When you're ineffective as watchman of your heart, you let the wrong people in, despite the walls you put up. Guard your heart, but ultimately allow God to be the Gatekeeper.
- As you move into a trusting relationship with God, He will show you the unhealthy ways you present yourself to the world.

- When your "no" becomes as important as your "yes," your life satisfaction will improve.
- True emotional maturity is realizing that although you've been a victim, in some instances, you were the perpetrator.
- Your attempts at loving others are unfruitful when you haven't practiced loving yourself.

# 7 | COME

Growing up, everyone knew when it was time for me to come in from playing outside. My mother would fling open the kitchen window and sing, "Liiiiiiiisaaaaaaa…"

I had an unwritten amount of time to get home. This was one of many unwritten rules of playing outside around the neighborhood. Like, I should be close enough to hear her. And if I was in someone's house, I should still hear her. If not, I should be well able to explain what I was doing inside their house.

If I were out of ear shot…Who am I kidding? I should never be out of ear shot.

How long was too long to respond to her call? Something like three minutes after the second call, if she had to call me a second time. Thankfully, friends and neighbors willingly participated in keeping me out of trouble most times. At any given moment around the time the sun dipped toward the west, if I missed the beckon, someone came running, "Your momma's calling you."

Whew! My grateful reply, "Good looking out."
I'd take off as fast as my feet or bike would fly, hoping to come in under the radar of the unspoken, unwritten, should've-known-better rule. Otherwise, there were consequences.

The purpose of the rules and the time limits were to help my mother ensure I was protected. As I got older, she trusted me with a bit more freedom. No matter my age or the time of day, when she called, it was time to come in. While my brave friends might defy their parents' wishes, I had two main reasons for obedience: avoid punishment (also known as the belt) and ensure I could enjoy freedom the next day.

In the puppy world, no such reasoning exists. When I called Hershey, he had no need, desire, or sense of urgency to avoid discipline. He probably didn't think that far ahead. His response generally centered on how my call measured up against the other immediate options and where we were in our relationship.

The more I understood his motivation, the more I could communicate what I wanted from him and set him up to win. He learned what I wanted while I learned what he liked. We grew to look more like a happy human/canine couple than a human with a stolen dog trying to escape her and get back home. Our growing relationship proved to go a long way toward getting to the best demonstration of reliability — the come command.

In my opinion, coming when called is the gold medal of dog and owner interaction. Remember trainer Debbie and her robot dog, Nigel? Remember how she said we should be the most important thing in our dog's life? Part of the reason is so they come immediately when called. I can't tell you exactly what else she said that day because it seemed so unlikely; I probably just tuned her out.

In our practice time at the park, Hershey would come for the hot dogs in my pocket. The catch — he had to either see me put them in there before we left, or see or smell them from where he stood. If he was playing with other dogs, running in the opposite direction, or sniffing something interesting, he pretended he didn't hear me calling. I would call, singing his name kind of like my mother did and he would keep right on running like I was some random crazy lady singing about chocolate. Since they clearly knew they weren't this "Hershey," I imagined the other dogs asking him if they knew who I was.

In my imagination, he answered no.

Sooner or later, when he was good and ready, Hershey sauntered over to me like nothing happened.

After watching Debbie with Nigel during puppy training each week, I believed she could work miracles. However, I wasn't sure she'd be able to help us with this one. I knew Hershey liked me, but it was asking a lot to think he'd willingly choose me over a stinky patch of God-knows-what or playing with other dogs.

Why is "come" a big deal in the dog world? If Hershey never got out accidentally and were never let off the leash to run free, everything would be fine, right? Basically, as long as he never had any freedom or fun, he'd be safe. What's the problem with that? A little boredom never hurt anybody.

Wrong attitude, Lisa.

Hershey was doing great in training, so why was I losing faith? Well, much of our training to that point depended on Hershey trusting me. But, come? Come required me to trust him. I had to let Hershey go and trust he would come back. Unhook his leash and trust he wouldn't run off permanently. Trust that no matter how much fun he was having, he'd respond to my call. Trust that I wouldn't be left alone holding the bag this time. I had some experience in that area which, I felt, gave me valid reason to fear.

One of my most memorable birthday parties was the year I turned 11 or 12. (You'll know in a moment why I can't remember how old I was). Your most memorable party was probably one where you had an amazing time. Mine was the one where no one came, except for my friend who came with me. And my stepsister, who also came with me.

The back story on the party is that my aunt lived about 10 minutes away from my neighborhood. Since she had a large, finished basement, we held my party at her house. Picture it. Music blaring, lights dim, and lots of food, plus about three people, not including the adults. Mortified, yet not terribly surprised. My party was on the same night as a party in my neighborhood. I supposed the reasons for my party being bare were the rain, the distance, and that everyone liked her better.

See, when we invite someone to a party, the idea is for the person to come. We hesitate to invite people we assume won't show up. We base our guest list on relationships. In other words, we deliberately play it safe.

Have you ever given up the possibility of something extraordinary in exchange for playing it safe? Like, not having another birthday party for nearly 20 years to avoid the potential for a similar rejection? (For any Oberlin friends, that surprise party for my 17th birthday in my college dorm room doesn't count. Thanks though).

To my credit, I wasn't willing to make Hershey play it safe. The dangers of a city puppy being loose were real; still, I couldn't imagine never letting him run free. For him, I decided to contend with 'what-if' scenarios and work with him through any mishaps. But we needed help. The section of Chicago where we lived had a high dog population, plus numerous cars and buses. We couldn't afford any of Hershey's tricks where he slipped out of his collar putting him in jeopardy.

I turned to a video, *Perfect Paws in 5 Days*, because it boasted many tools to "upgrade your dog's manners." After one lesson, I never picked it up again. I watched the lesson on "come" and decided the trainer, Jean Donaldson, was a genius.

First, the video suggested developing a special sound. I went overboard with this part. With Hershey sitting in front of me ready for training, I'd make a sound resembling a hybrid of a yodel and bird call to get his attention. Then, I handed over yummy treats for him basically just standing there. The idea was to associate the sound with the treats before using words.

Why a sound? In the heat of the moment, clarity is important because how you call affects the response you get. In case of emergency, there was no room for an angry or anxious tone to ruin Hershey's response. Additionally, sounds left no opportunity for confusion between the simple request "Come," and "Come. I said, Come. Come HERE. Get over here right now!"

We practiced several times a day, inside, away from danger or distractions, so Hershey could be off leash. Each time, I backed away a little so he had to come get the treat in response to the sound. Soon, we upped the ante and practiced off leash in our gated parking lot after walks. I'd leave him in a "stay" on one side of the lot and go to the other side and make the sound. Hershey would come running to get his treat. This technique worked like a charm. Hershey was learning to come the first time I called!

We soon got to test the technique in a real-world scenario. On a walk one day, I stopped to adjust Hershey's collar because we were approaching a park, and I wanted to be sure he was secure. Instead, I inadvertently let him loose. The escape artist took off like a lightning flash.

Rather than panic, I made our special "come" sound just as he rounded the corner halfway down the block. When he heard me, it was like he hit a wall. He stopped so abruptly that it resembled the cartoons where smoke would rise from the characters' feet when they stopped. Miraculously, Hershey followed the stop with an about-face and came charging back toward me even faster than when he ran away. When he reached me, he sat down and looked up like, 'Whatcha got?'

As you can imagine, I gave him every treat in one pocket and all the crumbs in the other. A dog owner who witnessed it all with her dog came over and asked how on earth I got him to respond like that. I explained the entire process...right after I got Hershey's leash back on. In the game called "Come," I finally got on the scoreboard.

Hershey 2,673, Lisa 1.

Have you been keeping score on how people in your life respond to your call? Do you know who answers quickly versus those who are tentative or never bother with a response?

Do your responses measure up, or are you out of balance? I was out of balance with most. And through my complaints of how I 'never get back what I put out,' I stretched my belt of hypocrisy nearly to the point of bursting. While demanding rushed responses from Hershey and increased frequency of responses from friends, I put forth delayed responses to God.

Why was it alright for me to postpone answering His calls? No excuse would suffice. Considering the personally tumultuous times surrounding Hershey's puppy years, I had more reason than ever to come to God.

The reasons for my hesitation long preceded Hershey. For starters, there was the irrational fear that washed over me from the inside whenever I heard my name called. I'd been avoiding "calls" for years because I immediately thought I was in trouble. Because I had trouble imagining something good on the other side of a call to "come," I ended up pressing pause on my emotional maturity.

As is usually the case when we stunt our growth, I hit some bumps on my journey. After years of misreading relational cues, I played certain mind games with myself as

I tried to get someone's attention. Like having the other half of a conversation when the other party either wasn't available or not interested in participating with me. Or, the game of pretending I only wanted friendship from someone I liked. Several times I hooked up guys I liked with someone I assumed they would like, rather than put myself on the line.

I had no faith in my ability to draw friends and companions to my side in a time of need or just to interact. Rather than depend on my magnetism, my remedy for companionship was to supply bait and treats to call people over to me. I perfected this tactic long before I got a puppy. While I didn't have ample finances to match my energy to bait and pursue, I was creative. I wrote love notes, shared sentiments through slow jam tapes, and did a few well-timed drive-by...uh, visits. I was that woman for years until God used Hershey to hold a mirror in front of me and later open my eyes to a new way to be.

No surprise that my aggressive and overbearing ways weren't reeling in new friends, especially boyfriends. Long time, well-meaning friends tried to point out the issues with my methods and introduce me to new tactics. I just wasn't getting it. The rules of engagement most folks employed in relationships didn't feel authentic to me. Cat and mouse games seemed juvenile, and my depleted esteem level didn't lend itself to 'letting him call me.'

There was another time in my 20s when a *boyfriend* (code for: he was my boyfriend, but I wasn't his girlfriend) told me that I didn't let him do anything in our relationship. Lisa of that day had little affiliation with signs demonstrating, 'he's just not that into you.' Even when his friends berated his treatment of me, nothing changed.

He insisted that when he would think about calling me, his phone rang with me on the other end. I termed it being forthright. Intentional, even. Making it known that I didn't play games. Nevertheless, my strategy, including the occasional drive-by, backfired. Most guys were as deaf to my cries for attention as I was to God's whispers of come. It was years before I got a clue.

Finally, I grew weary of my role as a type of relationship martyr and was done sacrificing my dreams and killing my desires for the sake of another person. Usually as I died in the relationship, my voice was often the first thing to go.

On the rare occasion that I spoke my desires, my tone didn't possess the authority I had over my body and time. The real crime? My so-called sacrifices rarely produced the result I imagined. What I wanted to do would never be as important as what they felt like doing. What I needed paled in comparison to what they wanted. My turn never came. When relationship after relationship ended, I was happy to believe that I was the one who missed it somewhere and caused the breach. Anything to maintain the illusion about my worth.

Truth was, I did miss it. Along the relationship path I asked for things before I was ready. I flirted before I knew how to comfortably entertain company, dated before using self-care routines to learn what I liked, and offered my body when I didn't know how to share my heart.

Therapy, mentorship, and prayer revealed that rectifying my destructive behavior would take more vulnerability on my part, not less. Even crying out to God had become a one-sided chase because I didn't trust Him enough to be still and await His presence to fill the voids and redefine my worth. "Quickie" worship encounters quenched my thirst temporarily. Yet God's desire was to bathe me in the deep waters of love that would end my quest for a love comparable to His.

God's depth of love for me came across as foreign because I believed Him to be a strict disciplinarian seeking perfection. When He called I wasn't in trouble, yet I hesitated. He wasn't asking for my hands or my service. He wanted my heart. He wanted time with me to go beyond healing my wounds. Without correcting my thinking about Him I could be healed, but not whole. Cue the chocolate canine therapist.

Hershey may not be a licensed therapy dog, but his cuddles were healing for me! They got me to slow down and just be. Because of him, I answered God's call and enjoyed quiet moments that didn't require me to do a thing except be adored.

Granted, I indulged Hershey in major ways. However, alongside our training and play times, we achieved an easy balance. I knew my worth in his life and didn't fear him changing his mind about it. The very things missing in my human interactions were present and working with my canine companion, but I had to make the connection.

Answers I needed for my life awaited me in my intimacy with God, but another missing link held me back.

Boundaries.

Doggie gates, crates, leashes, and tethers kept Hershey within safe boundaries every day. When he ventured outside those boundaries and moved toward danger, my voice called him back. Our growing relationship had boundaries fortifying its foundation because I held Hershey to a set of standards. What a revelation! To effectively train my soul for intimacy, I needed boundaries.

How would I start establishing boundaries? Time with God. I had to surrender. Willingly come to Him, lay it all down, trusting that my tears, fears, and mistakes wouldn't make Him turn away from me.

Eventually, Hershey surrendered too. Became more reliable to come when I called him. Don't get me wrong, I continued using treats, but they weren't a requirement.

Thankfully, as I weaned Hershey, he didn't turn around and run the other direction when he discovered I didn't have a treat for him. He accepted belly rubs or a scratch behind the ears instead. While affection required less investment, it more aptly fit our bond. It healed a part of my heart to have him express in small ways that I was enough.

What makes boundaries significant is the way they govern so we don't have to use control to bend someone's will. Boundaries leave room for choices that can either display love and respect or insult and neglect. Hershey's boundaries came in the form of training and my responses reinforced acceptable behavior. In time, he would even come to me when I was visibly angry. Slowly creeping in my direction he trusted me for the correction I love him enough to give.

Here again, Hershey expertly modeled an aspect of life I struggled in — trust. He showed up when I called even if he didn't know the outcome or couldn't see an immediate reward. If I just wanted to have him close, Hershey was good with that. He trusted me enough to come see what I wanted. Even after mistakes, he tiptoed toward me, submitted.

*Come.*

To begin my transition, fear had to go. Fear suffocated my relationships and prevented them from being free flowing exchanges. I took responsibility for failed relationships, but wasn't in tune enough with what constitutes wrong behavior to do something different. Nothing could change until I identified the specific issues. It terrified me to present myself, emotionally naked and vulnerable. Still, I couldn't keep running away. I had to be wholly present for the examination and participate in the change, no matter how safe and familiar my old ways felt.

No more sharing personal information, masking it as vulnerability while keeping my heart safely tucked away out of reach. In her book *Daring Greatly*, Brené Brown, PhD pulled the cover off that tactic when she said:

> "I define vulnerability as uncertainty, risk and emotional exposure. With that definition in mind, let's think about love. Waking up every day and loving someone who may or may not love us back, whose safety we can't ensure, who may stay in our lives or may leave without a moment's notice, who may be loyal to the day they die or betray us tomorrow — that's vulnerability."[3]

As humans, we can't wholeheartedly participate in relationships where fear and pride are laid out like a beautiful tablecloth, but vulnerability isn't on the table. When

---

[3] Brené Brown, *Daring Greatly: How the Courage to Be Vulnerable Transforms the Way We Live, Love, Parent, and Lead. Penguin Publishing Group. Kindle Edition,* p. 34

discomfort hits, pride generally says, 'I'm not trying that ever again.' It keeps track of everything we're afraid will expose our hearts. To show up vulnerable takes faith and courage. No gifts or gimmicks to hide behind – just you. When I could do that, my relationships intensified.

God faithfully meets us when we come to him without pride, blame, or false humility. When we're truly open we come without portraying ourselves as any better or worse than we actually are. And when we operate within the boundaries of people, places, and things that He's set up we can expect an invitation to come even closer.

When our hearts and time are free of false pretenses and idols we can achieve true intimacy. Once my focus shifted from how other people failed me to how I could please Him and fulfill His purpose for my life, I came to Him — arms wide — without waiting for Him to call. He began to heal the broken places lying to me about what I deserved. It all began with, "Come."

It took time, but finally, I laid the heaviness of broken and strained relationships at His feet. As newly developed boundaries and standards governed my relationships, I found new joy.

God wants us to bring our pain, burdens, and mistakes when He calls for us to come.

Sometimes, He simply wants to share our time, attention, and space. Spending time with Him in close proximity delivered my best introduction to intimacy.

Our Heavenly Father loves when we exhibit full surrender and trust in Him. He's not as put off by the number of times we miss it as He is by a lack of faith in His loving commitment to us.

I was nearly 40 before I fully embraced the disservice I did my friends who I wouldn't disagree with or express to them my need for an exchange. While I thought I was keeping peace and being low-drama, I allowed people I said I loved to go into the world with unchecked behaviors and ideas. Though I was unwilling to subject the world to an undisciplined dog, I was fully aware these people could be hurtful and undisciplined.

As I got older, my fear of rejection morphed into the idea that I wasn't qualified to address certain issues because of past failures or present circumstances. Addressing the issue was within my reach, but I didn't want to rock the boat. How selfish! This is what happens when we don't acknowledge that fear and love can't co-exist. While claiming to be forgotten and unloved, I let fear drive me. I wouldn't allow Hershey to travel beyond certain boundaries because I loved him. Where was that love for my friends or myself?

I thought I was walking out the adage of treating others how I wanted them to treat me when I was really doing the opposite! I moaned about shallow relationships, ignorant to the fact that I dictate the depth of the relationships in part by my willingness to maintain my voice. Every day, Hershey reminds me that boundaries and lack of agreement don't equate to absence of love. He also illustrates that I don't have to fear love being withheld in response to my truth.

I've learned to rest in the acceptance I feel in coming to God whether I'm in a tough emotional battle, or things are good. I'm better at rejecting thoughts and memories that bring shame. I don't feel the need to always be "on" in order to be accepted by people, and my time with God makes me a much better friend.

Do you have an area in your life where you're reluctant to come out of your shell? Do new acquaintances and old friends all seem to say the same things about how you interact?

You may be in a great place with no visible evidence of poor choices. Or, you may wake each morning greeted with the stress of consequences overflowing in every area of your life. The beauty is that God doesn't have favorites based on what people can see. When we come, sometimes crouching low under the weight of burdens we're ill-equipped to carry, He's looking at our hearts. We have a place at God's feet and at His table. You get to choose where you want to sit, but first, you have to respond.

How? Making time and getting quiet are great places

to start.

If you purpose to come, you'll be surprised at how you begin to hear God when He speaks. Decide today to reject the pride keeping you so focused on your emotions that you miss the cues your environment presents.

God orchestrates our lives in ways that we learn from Him and the people who cross our path. When we don't pay attention to either, we run the risk of missing out on our best growth and sharpening opportunities.

What then? You end up learning life lessons from your pet!

So, perhaps you're in transition and seeing minimal results. Are the people around you transferring confusion or peace? And what should you consider if you can't hear the whispers of God over the screams of your heart?

I suggest you clear your surroundings of shame reminders (which may include some people). Shame indicates fear is present, which also blocks communication with God. Shame reminders lessen your ability to think and see bigger than your current circumstances.

Time with God is a faith builder and helps develop communication with Him and evict fear and shame. When He calls, come.

Reject the idea that responding to Him can wait until a more convenient time. Once He begins tugging on your heart, there's nothing more important on your schedule.

When you've done something yet again that you wish you hadn't, don't run. There's nowhere to hide. Just come. Allow His love and grace to remind you that temptation always has an escape.

Come even after a friend turns her back and you can't figure out why. Run to God and tell Him about your anger and confusion. Tell Him how you don't ever want to feel this way again.

In those painful moments, ask God to make you aware of judgments and triggers that awaken your insecurities, and the people who stir them. Practice your responses in advance. Be vigilant and choose peace by any means necessary.

If the relationships don't change, courageously change your relationships.

Together, let's come to Him for all our emotional needs. Let's opt for the peaceful freedom of casting our cares on Him.

### Soul Training Tips

- We give up major opportunities to learn and grow when we constantly play it safe.
- How we 'call' affects the response we get.
- God is waiting for us to end our quest to find love comparable to His.

- The best relationships are those with boundaries strengthening the foundation.
- Our relationships aren't wholehearted if fear and pride are laid out like a beautiful tablecloth, but vulnerability isn't on the table.
- Time with God can make us aware of judgments and triggers that make us insecure.

# 8 | GOOD BOY

I am fully persuaded my life is better, in part, because of Hershey. In the beginning, he was something to love and to love me, satisfying an ache I carried since childhood. Running after accolades and applause from teachers and peers, I never really got around to answering the call of my soul. Landing in church opened the door to truths necessary to root out my soul's issues, but I kept dancing around the process. Hershey modeled an excellent training pupil, helping me see clearly to being one, too.

I watched my resilient canine adapt to our change of family dynamics, scenery, and living quarters with ease. Having me near seemed enough to keep him content. Oh, and food. And something that squeaks. And a ball.

Soon, Hershey became my motivation. He moved into the role of trainer and gave me a reason to want to win. As crazy as it sounds, he began training me on how to live again.

Besides the relational importance of soul training, through it, I also learned how misleading talents and gifts can be. God desires that we reconcile our issues long before we ever hit any version of platform or stage. Whether you're a teacher in a classroom, a preacher in the pulpit, or a politician at the podium, the time to uncover bad habits and unhealthy tendencies is *before* mounting those platforms.

When scandals erupt, the world condemns the behavior that's been exposed, but only a few consider where that behavior began. In my training process, I had to look back on all the things I did. Acknowledge how low some of my behaviors went, and the people hurt by them. Further, I needed to expose, to someone I trusted, the secret pains no one knew about that fueled many of those behaviors. That raw exchange lit the path toward wholeness, in part by making repentance easy. It's hard to turn away from what you're unwilling to admit.

Somehow, communicating with Hershey awakened a part of me that wanted to be seen and heard and understood. Yet, the idea of opening up provoked a cold sweat. I rejected every part of the "into me see" of intimacy because I wasn't sure what was in there or how to lead anyone to it. For me, a therapist and mentor answered the call to get it out.

Once things are laid out on the table, we get the choice of whether or not to eat them. While they remain hidden in our pockets and purses, we carry them around getting fat and sick, as if we don't know why. Find someone with whom you can empty your pockets. Dump your purse and sift through the items. Scream. Cry.

Be careful to not get stuck in regret. Ask for forgiveness. Be prepared for those who forgive, but don't let you back in.

Looking back can be hard. For the record, I did some dumb stuff. Like, really dumb. I'm here and whole today because I didn't quit. I never believed my destiny was to only do dumb things. With help to do better and be better, I knew I would.

Many times, our goals focus on what we want to accomplish or achieve instead of who we want to be when we hit those targets. For me, soul training was about maximizing my potential for the way I live, which includes my behaviors and relationships, not just what I do. Becoming who I wanted to be required me to evaluate the way I did things. I wanted the madness to stop, so I had to stop the madness.

Enter Hershey.

He changed me in many ways that I hear babies change moms. I'm less selfish, I get up earlier than I want to, and I'm obsessed with sharing pictures and stories about little things he does. He can get on my nerves when I'm with him, but I miss him terribly when we're apart. And, I'd fight a bear to protect him.

Hershey impacted the parts of my heart and emotions that I liked to pretend didn't matter. I could see him struggle when he couldn't understand what I wanted. Rather than walk away, he would just try *something*. Usually, he tried a little of everything, running through his repertoire of tricks and commands in hopes he'd get to it. I didn't know how much I ached to see someone make the effort.

Hershey also had a gift of uncovering my heart posture, no matter how deep I believed it was buried. I got the idea for this book when I realized I studied, practiced, and strived to communicate with an animal, but had given up on seeing eye to eye with my former spouse.

Out of love, I created a way for Hershey and I to understand each other. When he had an accident on the floor (and that one time he vomited on my bed), I forgave quickly. I didn't hold infractions over his head or punish him repeatedly for the same offense. Most of all, I didn't withhold what I knew he liked because of something he did last week. I started him over fresh each time.

I'm embarrassed to admit that bruised pride mixed with feelings of rejection fueled the exact opposite responses in my earlier marriage. I let offenses build up on top of my brokenness. Now I know better, and grace gives me permission and the power to do better and be better. Again.

When people asked how I could get married again, it's the same reason I make new friends. I don't live a life of blame, shifting all the responsibility for issues to the other person. I focus on the girl in the mirror and assess what she could've done differently. I move forward from that place, determined to try harder next time to find my people and steward them well.

Today, my marriage isn't perfect, but it's real. What I bring to the table is from a whole woman versus a girl bound by her insecurities and driven by her fears. It's not about comparing him to anyone. What we have feels different mostly because I'm different. Every day, I practice being fully present, fully me.

When we first moved into our current home, we didn't have any full length mirrors. One day, my husband grabbed an inexpensive one and put it behind our bedroom door. As someone who formerly struggled with weight, I was leery of mirrors. But this one was pretty flattering. Too flattering. In this mirror, my problem areas were camouflaged. Magical, right? Wrong. Rather than allow that mirror to lull me into a false sense of security where I could eat anything I wanted, I decided to use the other mirrors in the house to keep me on my toes.

Unfortunately, when we wear masks with our friends and loved ones, they're like that mirror. What they reflect back to us is flattering, but it's not true. We can't ensure we're availing ourselves to the sharpening God intended to be done by our friends unless we're authentic. I wore masks for so long in efforts to please people that I lost who I was and a sensitivity to my needs. I no longer knew what I liked, couldn't articulate what I wanted, and was too fearful to express my needs. No more.

Though I feel I look best in sunlight and candlelight because of the flattering shadows they cast, Hershey flicked on every light in my life. Add to that, he propped up mirrors that reflected every angle. When I yelled at him because I was tired or too chicken to yell at who I was really mad at, there was the mirror. His hazel eyes grew sad and he'd come up and start licking my arm or my leg, his way of apologizing though we both knew he didn't do anything wrong. In those moments, I saw myself — every unflattering roll, unwanted chin hair, and even that light mustache. I didn't like what I saw, so I got to work.

Part of the reason I love being around Hershey is he loves being with me. As if he can really comprehend the ways I attempt to show him love, he's excited to see me when I come in. Granted, he often wants to play or get a belly rub. After that's over, he simply chills out in my presence. I love to hear him exhale and see him peacefully resting, believing I had a hand in it. Although, I'm sure living with me wasn't always easy.

As I underwent grueling emotional transformation, foul moods would come and go. Hershey never changed toward me. When I struggled and took my frustration out on him, he didn't hold a grudge. He was a faithful companion, despite being a reflection for so many of my flaws. He served as a proxy, demonstrating I'm worth the extra effort needed to love me. He patiently led me into wholeness and authenticity by showing me I could get it wrong, without having to fear abandonment. Sure, he was a dog without a lot of options, but we all know there are ways to express disillusionment without leaving!

Furthermore, Hershey seemed to expect me to get it right, which was a great motivator to either get it right or repent quickly when I didn't. Even when he grew more independent, we didn't grow apart. For these reasons and many more, Hershey will always be worthy of the phrase, "Good boy."

Television trainers and old-school dog owners caution against too much praise and dog treats. I can't say I ever fully bought into their reasons, other than wanting to make sure our doggies don't get too fat. Their cautions didn't make me stop using treats; they simply made me change treats and how I gave them. After all, what Hershey offered me was more than obedience, so how could I diminish his reward? All the treats, fun walks, comfy beds, and squeaky toys in the world couldn't repay him for what he walked me through.

Hershey was the reason I got out of the house every day no matter what I felt like. Many times, all I wanted to do was stare at the wall wondering where it all went wrong. But for him, I went out several times a day. I may not have showered or put on make-up, but I got up and out. The pizzas and cookies I consumed would've taken me over had it not been for those walks.

Like a best friend, Hershey saw what no one else saw and communicated truth in a way that's unique to us. In return, I'm committed to caring for him in the ways he can't care for himself. Not just because he is a dog, but because he is *my* dog. He didn't show up on my doorstep. I brought him home, and he didn't have any say in the matter. So even if I have a sad day, he gets the same walks he does when I'm happy to give them.

If you're anything like I was inside, your heart and intentions may be pure while many of your relationships reflect a flawed execution of self-love, and how you love others. Like me, maybe you need an aspect of soul training to exercise love muscles you haven't been using. The ones where you speak your truth, including your needs, and stand firm in the belief that you deserve what you request. Walking out each of the soul training commands helped me develop better relational methods and behaviors.

Today, I can acknowledge that the love of God is not only far reaching, but creative. God desires for us to live whole, full lives. To live that out, we must embrace accountability, including holding others accountable and responsible for loving us well, overlooking our collective imperfections. Being unfulfilled and consistently ignoring my needs wasn't God's best for my life. As my Father, He knew the way to get me to bend; He used a puppy to break down my defenses!

My encouragement to you is to not shy away from looking closely at your surroundings. There's likely a person, place, or animal in your environment that can expand or reshape your thinking in an area of your life. How can you be accountable for change without a complete picture of your current state and a path in the direction of where you need to go? Hershey lit that path for me. To find your path, you must recognize how God is dealing with you and welcome His methods.

Hershey was the catalyst to open my heart to "doing the work." It was imperative to work on my life with the same enthusiasm I have in relation to him. My therapist and mentors came along to translate each of my lessons into a life of authentic faith along with self-awareness and self-care. They also helped recalibrate my relationship with Hershey so I could tear myself away from him and get out to practice letting people in again.

Once I started making connections, the mind fog lifted. However, it became important for me not to abandon Hershey. I wanted to share the happy, emotionally balanced Lisa with him to contrast the bad days he endured with me. By the time my husband Jeffrey came into our lives, Hershey and I were both ready for a new start.

Although Jeffrey wasn't a self-proclaimed dog person, almost immediately, he and Hershey began to develop their own relationship. After living and sleeping with just me for years, I thought Hershey would resent the new set-up, especially being relegated to his own beds. Yet, he handled the new rules and our move like a trooper! If there's a way to train for transition, I'd say we did it.

Years later, Hershey and I remain on track, and we've adjusted to life as a party of three. We still have our special communication, and he's living the good life of a healthy senior dog in Florida. And, when Jeff's out of town, he may or may not get to sleep on the couch.

In the beginning, my reasons for training Hershey were more about him. In the end, I believe I got the most benefit. I hope our story encourages you to look more closely at your approach to love, relationships, and self-care. The key for me to become whole once I discovered how God wanted to deal with me, was to fully participate in the process.

Though Hershey and I have our own way of communicating, I try to teach any newcomers the ropes about how to walk through some of his commands. I let them know that "okay" is one of our release words. After he obeys and can be released for his reward, saying "okay" helps him understand that he passed the test.

Further confirmation of a job well done was hearing the oft-used: "Good boy." This became his cue that either a toy, yummy treat, or some behind the ear scratches and belly rubs were on deck.

"Good boy" is a chorus around these parts. As his person and his trainer, I can say Hershey truly embodies the phrase.

My ultimate goal? To remember my main objective: do good works and glorify God with my life. Part of that is remembering that He's as invested in who I **am** as what I do. Therefore, the type of friend, employee or business owner I am, the way I manage my family, and even how I care for my animal are all important to Him.

Why bother working so hard? Because I'm an extension of Him in the earth. And, I long to hear Him whisper, *Good girl.*

# ACKNOWLEDGMENTS

This labor of love was a long time in the making with many hands and hearts involved. Whether you read one of the many drafts, or simply asked about it, you're appreciated! Most of all, I wish to acknowledge God and thank Him for sending the most amazing, patient, supportive husband in Jeffrey (I love you!), and the best dog in the whole world to come and train me.

Special thanks to my editor, Dr. Vernetta Williams, and graphic designers Jacqueline Jones (cover) and Trevell Southall. And to my sister-friend Ruth S. Southall who did a little of everything to help push this baby out, I love you sooo much!

Pastor Sandra Howell, your ability to cultivate gifts and purpose is extraordinary. I'm not sure whether I'm more grateful for the way you poured into me (including any "re-direction," lol), or the confidence you currently show in what you know you helped develop in me. I pray I can pay it forward with even a measure of the grace and effectiveness you did. I love you!

A heartfelt thanks to the Pastors, Leaders and church families who covered me throughout the years. I'm thankful God allowed a season with each of you; I'm forever changed by the ministry I received at your hands. Tabernacle of God COGIC, Progressive Life-Giving Word Cathedral, Family Harvest, New Life Covenant, (Pastor Hannah, I got my LIFE at New Life!) Epistle of Christ Ministries & World Champions, I love you ALL!

Thanks to my brothers & sisters on both sides, my Mother & also Daddy (in heaven), natural & spiritual families (including the Williams, Caillouette, Richmond, Mitchell, Banks, Hurt, Ladson, Payne & Surrett folks), mentors, and lifelong friends who endured the old and new me, plus the girl in the middle who was still working it all out. Much love!

# ABOUT THE AUTHOR

Lisa is a Christ follower, wife to Jeffrey, dog mom, ordained minister, teacher, writer, speaker and…more than a conqueror!

Created to encourage and exhort, Lisa is a certified coach and mentor, passionate about helping women navigate the path to their dreams and embrace the journey along the way. In addition to writing and blogging, Lisa hosts events to encourage personal growth and help others to recognize and cultivate their gifts. She spearheaded a conference called The S.P.A. Experience, a movement designed to be a place of respite, connection, and belonging. At SPA, ladies can share, pray and affirm each other while enjoying a unique worship experience.

Beyond that Lisa is committed to being a lifelong learner and continuing to seek after wisdom and direction to fulfill her purpose. In addition to it all, she relishes having a life that includes real love, real friends, and really good laughs!

To inquire about booking Lisa to speak at your next event, email info@lifewithlisae.com.